PRAISE FOR BRIGHTENING GLANCE

"A portrait of the artist as a woman working and living in the heart of the downtown New York art world. Pat Lipsky's book is a stylish, entertaining, and, above all, honest memoir of a painter's life and times. If you wondered what it would really have been like to be an artist in the years when art was all about art, this book opens the door."
—LOUIS MENAND, contributor to *The New Yorker* and Pulitzer–Prize winning author, *The Metaphysical Club: A Story of Ideas in America*

"How did Pat Lipsky pull off the near-impossible feat of breaking into the hyper-macho downtown art world? She tells us in *Brightening Glance*. With this memoir, Lipsky proves that she's as brilliant, energetic, and brave a writer as she is a painter."
—LILI ANOLIK, contributing editor to *Vanity Fair* and *Air Mail,* author, *Didion & Babitz*

"From fisticuffs at Max's Kansas City between Andy Warhol's flamboyant entourage and Carl Andre's minimalist cadre to the secret confessions of über-critic Clement Greenberg, *Brightening Glance* is a shockingly candid art world exposé by a talented painter who has survived more than five decades of culture wars. As both protagonist and witness, Lipsky lays bare the vanities of the artists, dealers, and critics who made the late twentieth century art scene in New York the fulcrum of artistic innovation and ideological rivalry amidst chaotic private lives. Lipsky spares no one from her acid pen, least of all herself."
—MICHAEL FINDLAY, author, *Portrait of the Art Dealer as a Young Man: New York in the Sixties*

"*Brightening Glance* is an intense, deeply moving memoir about the New York art world, what it was, what it's become, and what it means to have a sensibility and talent that doesn't always fit the age. It will touch anyone who loves painting and who can find salvation in museums and galleries. Filled with characters, incident, and the excitement of the city at night, Lipsky's book is balanced at that place where life becomes art."
—RICH COHEN, *New York Times* bestselling author
and contributing editor to *Rolling Stone*

"Here is an artist memoir of SoHo grit and thrown punches, of bad divorces and career reversals. What sets *Brightening Glance* apart is the sensitivity of its observations. A praised abstractionist on canvas, Pat Lipsky on paper proves to be a sensitive portraitist, with an astonishing command of the figures who surrounded her. Tony Smith, Lee Krasner, Clement Greenberg, Andy Warhol, Robert Smithson, and Pierre Rosenberg, among many others, leap off the page in this bittersweet and at times challenging depiction of art, love, and life."
—JAMES PANERO, executive editor at *The New Criterion*

BRIGHTENING
GLANCE

BRIGHTENING GLANCE

Art and Life

PAT LIPSKY

UNIVERSITY OF IOWA PRESS, IOWA CITY

University of Iowa Press, Iowa City 52242
Copyright © 2025 by Pat Lipsky

uipress.uiowa.edu
ISBN: 978-1-68597-034-5 (cloth)
ISBN: 978-1-68597-023-9 (ebook)
Printed in the United States of America

Design by Karen Copp
Typesetting by Rebecca Evans

Some of the names and identifying details of people mentioned
in this book have been changed.

Printed on acid-free paper

Cataloging-in-Publication data is on file with the Library of
congress.

Henri Matisse epigraph page vii: "Il faut regarder toute sa vie avec
des yeux d'enfants," *Le Courrier de l'U.N.E.S.C.O.*, vol. VI, n°10;
translated in *Art News and Review*, February 6, 1954, p. 3.

In memory of my father,
Bernard George Sutton,
who walked with his head facing the sky.

The reality I have known no longer exists.
The places we have known do not belong solely to
the world of space in which we situate them for our
greater convenience. They were only a thin slice
among contiguous impressions which formed our
life at that time; the memory of a certain image
is but regret for a certain moment . . .
—MARCEL PROUST, *Swann's Way*

Was it a vision, or a waking dream?
—JOHN KEATS, "Ode to a Nightingale"

The effort needed to see things without distortion
takes something very like courage . . .
—HENRI MATISSE

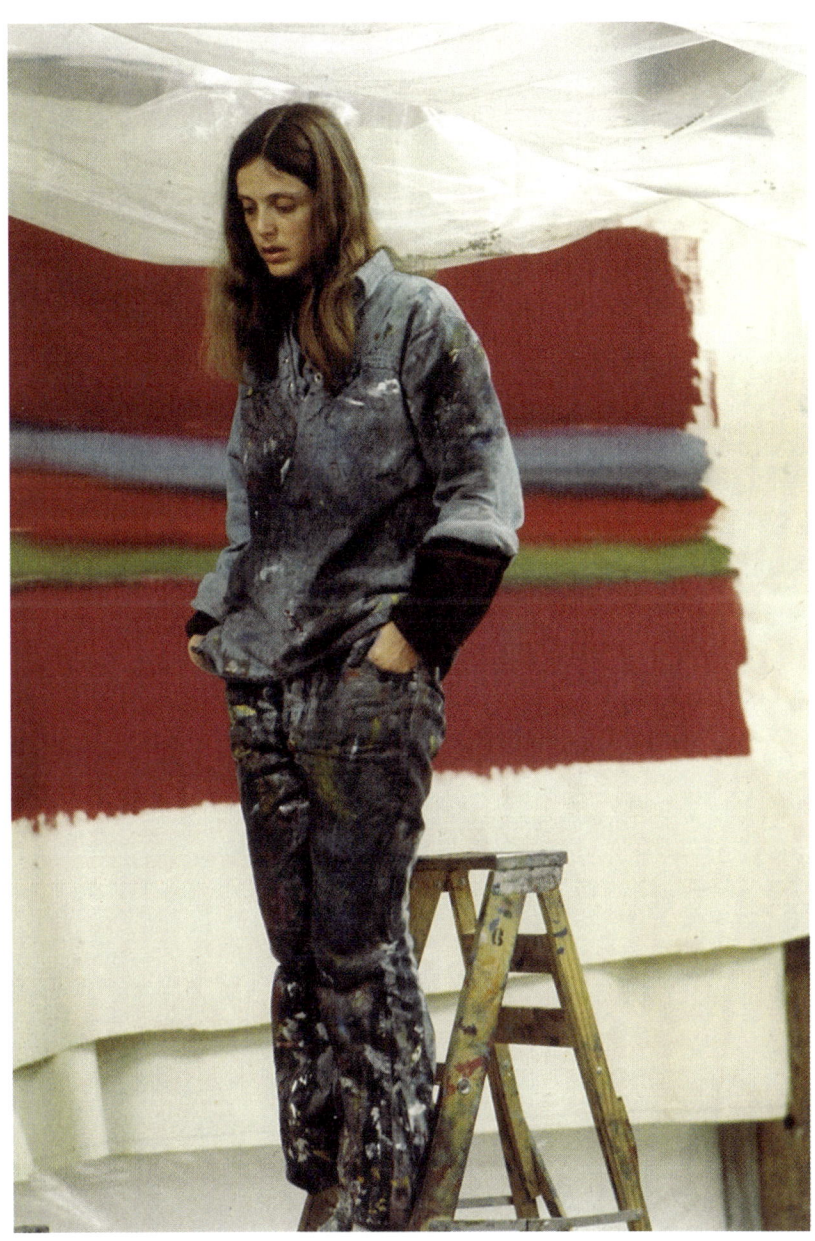

In my Hoosick Falls studio, 1971.

CONTENTS

BRIGHTENING GLANCE

PREFACE

CHANCE, LIKE NEGATIVE SPACE in a painting or silence between notes, is as important in what happens as what is willfully planned. In early September 1964 I was on the Upper East Side of Manhattan, in the building that housed Hunter College's Department of Art and Art History. My initial attempt to register for Advanced Painting had been thwarted by the department secretary, a stickler for details. Then I noticed Ray Parker, dressed in a professional tweed sports jacket, standing to the side. Parker was a color field painter who showed his work regularly on Fifty-Seventh Street. I didn't know anything about him, though, just that he probably was a professor. So I got my courage up and asked *him* to sign me into the class that, coincidentally, he was teaching. And he did.

AND THAT CHANGED EVERYTHING.

I was born in 1941 in New York City. Secretly, I've always believed the tensions of World War II seeped into my baby formula. It took four grueling years for our side to win. One of my earliest memories is celebrating that victory: a group of kids marching around my Brooklyn neighborhood banging pots. And within months, America was in the Cold War and soon after that the McCarthy era began. In school there were weekly "duck and cover" drills: at the sound of a gong we'd cradle our head in our arms and dive under our desks, dog tags jangling. Our names and ID numbers were inscribed in metal so our charred bodies could be identified once the atom bomb dropped. My parents told me *never* to say the word "Russia" in public. Even the word "red" was suspect and to be avoided.

In the sixties I became an adult. At the same time many of the barriers and taboos we'd grown up with slipped away. Things started well enough when John F. Kennedy—Ivy League, chic, and expounding the liberal views we'd just learned in college—was elected president. Who could have predicted that within three years he'd be assassinated in Dallas, Texas. The country, or at least the East Coast, was reeling. But it turned out to be only a beginning—followed by the assassinations of the Reverend Martin Luther King and Robert Kennedy in 1968. Surely some Second Coming was at hand. By the late sixties the floodgates had opened: sex, divorce, drugs—everyone high on LSD. Protocols like respect for your elders had vanished. We were all on a first-name basis. And that's the backdrop for *Brightening Glance*. Bob Dylan nailed it when he sang, "The times they are a-changin'."

And for me too. Married in 1962, I had two children in quick succession, then attended graduate school in painting. The biggest surprise came in 1969 when I went from pushing a stroller around Carl Schurz Park to showing my pictures in one of the best galleries in town. I was twenty-eight and for a whole year high on success.

NEW YORK CITY is a tough town where real estate and money often dictate what is possible. Following Edna St. Vincent Millay, Robert Frost, Djuna Barnes, and other bohemian writers from the 1920s, Greenwich Village continued to be the avant-garde destination in the 1940s and '50s. Jackson Pollock, Clement Greenberg, James Baldwin, and Willem de Kooning all lived and worked in the Village, as well as the French émigré surrealist André Breton. By the time my generation came along, the Village was too expensive and its spaces too small. The legacy we'd received from Abstract Expressionism was to continue creating wall-size abstract pictures. And for young steel sculptors emulating David Smith, it was to build out and weld, also putting space at a premium. A 1962 report referred to the area south of Houston as the wasteland of New York. To which, because of its low rents and huge expanses, contemporary painters and sculptors started moving. There was simply no other place to go.

We pioneered the neighborhood—forged and wall-removed live-work lofts out of abandoned factories, everyone covered in sawdust. We had taken that old factory history and turned it into play—a different architectural sort of masquerading. It became the new frontier. And when my former husband said no, he wasn't up for the move, it was just me and my two sons who entered the three-thousand-square-foot loft at 42 Wooster.

Not that many women lived in the neighborhood then. And it wasn't especially safe either.

Despite that, living in SoHo was spectacular. It's what I imagine Florence might have been like during the early Renaissance when artists, architects, and philosophers lived within walking distance of one another. Or, in our time, like being on an avant-garde college campus for artists. You knew most everyone, so strolling down the street became one long, ongoing conversation: about sales, the work, upcoming parties, openings, and who was dating whom. New galleries cropped up, which you could drop into on the way for coffee or a drink. Our spaces were huge and stark, our lives uninhibited. And in a short time, some of the wealthy who came down to look at and acquire our artwork became covetous of our lofts and way of life. They wanted to reap the rewards of what we'd sown. And before we knew it, they had pushed us out.

PROUST ONCE WROTE that the unexplored parts of our lives are like negatives waiting to be developed. In this book I've set out to develop those negatives, to give form to my life as a painter from the late sixties on. Endemic to the art world is the moment when the scene shifts and taste changes. As a result of chance, your group is now out. The attention lasted for a time—until it didn't. In *Brightening Glance* I've tried to capture the images of those years before they are lost in the ether.

LADY IN A HAT

THIS WOMAN WITH A GREAT FIGURE walks into my painting class. Luscious lips, tiny nose. It's the first day of the term. Floral silk shirt, matching skirt, and lots of jewelry; she's wildly overdressed. The gold sandals show off her perfect pedicure.

When I ask her name she answers, "Annika." And, to the obvious follow-up: "Kazakhstan."

Everything I know about this part of the world comes from Chekhov. If I meet someone from Moscow, I try to see them as one of those philandering Petersburgians. If they're from Kiev, I think about them cheating on their spouses in Odessa. Russians of my acquaintance talk about winter, and all I can picture is snowy streets forded by droshkies. To be in the arts is to encounter the world through art; that is, colorful and populated, and also frequently wrong.

"What are you planning," I ask, "to do in this class?"

"Pastels," she says. "I want to work in pastels. These." She points to the three large unopened boxes of colored chalk she's brought.

I tell her that particular kind won't mix very well. Other people in class are looking at us.

The main thing about a painting class atmosphere: it's nosy. Everybody wants to pick up that little bit extra. "What about using paint?" I ask.

Annika answers in this weirdly resolute way, as if we've argued and she is releasing us from argument. "I'll think about it."

Teaching in this respect is like being a doctor: you need to know their history. What they've looked at, any visual and stylistic contagions, germs they might've picked up, immunities that can still develop. It makes painting feel more teachable—and it gives the students confidence.

Annika has never studied painting before. "I work as a model. I even tried to model here, but they wouldn't take me."

Unlike many foreign students, she speaks English without grammatical errors. She's not wearing a smock—it may be why she's chosen pastel, a relatively neat medium. "You might want a smock, or something. They sell them in the art store." When she smiles again I notice the high-gloss lipstick on her thick lips.

AN HOUR LATER she's drawing a design using interlocking wavy shapes. It looks, at best, like a fabric pattern: at worst, a colored doodle in a student's notebook. She's executed it with two pastels—viridian green, cerulean blue. Secretly I write Annika off. The room is crowded and there are other students to get through before the end of session.

People whose life is incomplete without art have no idea what a life filled with art, complete with art, mostly or only art, is like. These young people right out of college who suddenly decide to take up painting. A few who escape boring jobs a couple days a week; older, retired people who now think they should've studied painting all along; always a few dropouts—college or grad school last-chancers—trying to resurrect themselves. A lot of them have talent. But it takes way more than talent to succeed. Some people, here as elsewhere, succeed without talent. A name, or some quirk of timing. One woman from my class had a famous last name. Now she's showing her trivial pictures in both Santa Fe and Miami. While the others continue on, stoically unexhibited.

Three new students arrive at the class's second meeting. One Iowan, two from South Korea. Nothing special.

There are no requirements for admission, so I don't really know who will show up. After intake conversations, I'm ready to look at the work of my regulars. I pretty much know where they are in the room because people in an art class are territorial: if at all possible they want to return to the same place they worked in before. It could be for luck, maybe also for comfort. It's never discussed.

I sit with each student and their work and we talk about it. We diagnose it. Today Annika is wearing a straw hat similar to, but smaller than, the memorable one sported by Adélaïde Labille-Guiard in her 1785 *Self-Portrait with Two Pupils*. That's one of the ways you end up seeing the world: fashion as a wormhole into these personalities and fashions you know from the museums. People who have become real to you as people. But Labille-Guiard's hat is topped with a large bow. I also notice Annika's smock.

On her easel sits a small finished canvas. At its center there's a sort of Roman bust—a man's head, bull neck, meaty shoulders, and upper torso. The figure's hair and cruel, twisted smile aren't painted in naturalistic color. Its blues and greens make the whole composition look intertwined, internal, and sinister—a person seen through a force of fear, envy, obstructed adulation.

As I walk toward Annika, she wiggles her right index finger to show me it's now blue.

"If you're using your finger to apply paint, that's okay," I say. "In art all that matters is the result." I don't know how true this is—or rather, it's true of the work, though the artists can still disappoint you. I think she must really like the color blue.

The man's facial expression is quizzical and slightly crooked, head turned partially from the viewer. The image could double as an illustration for Kafka's *The Metamorphosis*—Gregor Samsa, pre-bug. Annika has managed something most students can't do: to make a unified picture.

"It's terrific," I say.

She looks pleased.

So, I was wrong about Annika. She made a good painting, and even on the second day. Art is like that too.

I keep glancing at her small nose. I am intrigued and wonder how she could breathe through such tiny nostrils. These lips are too charismatic. There's just something about her that's always *over*. I've been involved with art for half a century, and my sense of amount is one thing that's become developed.

Sometimes a few students will congregate in front of the picture being discussed. The more students, the more interesting it seems. They rush over. It's selfishness, bargain hunting, New Yorkers' desire: they want more art.

This canvas seems to have been done by someone with lots of experience. "I thought you said you never painted before," I say.

She looks down.

"Where'd you get the idea?" I do not want to embarrass her. I think she's going to say her inspiration came from that vast Russian steppe. (In the four days since her first class, I have gone back and reread Chekhov.)

While American children—like my kids—watched TV and played video games, Annika had drawn nourishment from the exotic Kazakhstanian landscape.

"Is this broken-plate treatment an image from your childhood?" I ask. And Annika's laugh parts her shiny lips.

"Actually I am here over twenty years," she tells me.

"Sure. Still it's visually different, and your childhood landscape must be embedded in your unconscious."

Her not agreeing seems pouty and spoiled. There is a certain kind of student who wants to embarrass you. To dispute. Annika is of this number. "Not really. I hardly ever played outside. I like this pattern."

And then, from the other side of the room, a student—twenty-five, one of the self-resurrectors—cups his hand and yells, "Schnabel, it looks like a Schnabel—you know, the broken plates."

There's a pause. Then Annika, smiling, says, "Oh yes. I know Julian."

It was funny we already had a rapport. "I've always thought he looked like a butcher, " I say.

Annika giggles. "Oh, but it is his *father* who was the butcher."

I understand what she must be. Schnabel's girlfriend, or ex. No surprise. A lot of aging painters' former lovers wander the city. Women and men often disoriented by creativity. It's a hard thing, touching art. People who can turn an object, their talent to acclaim, into tangible money. How do you go back to ordinary life after seeing that? And there is that hard tradition for male painters—one you notice even in your peers, even in men who swore this would not be them—starting to date models the evening they turn sixty.

What's funny is that Annika's small unassuming picture is *better* than Schnabel.

But of course the idea, constructing a picture out of shards, was his. Without it she'd have no image to start from. This is why the innovator gets the credit.

"It was a few years ago, and now Julian lives with someone else." It sounds painful, and she's *not* smiling.

I ask, just to verify my own data, "How old is Schnabel?"

Annika answers, "Sixty-four." She follows with the hackneyed phrase, the tried and untrue, "We are still friends."

This leaves her sentence just sitting there in the ward. Unbandaged, quiet on the gurney. To doctor that up, she continues, "He told me if I ever have a show, he will come to see it."

"That's really great of him," I respond with enthusiasm. "Why doesn't he try to *get* you a show?"

Annika changes topics. "Julian did some paintings of me." Pulling out her phone she scrolls down to three tiny images. A nondescript blond woman standing in the middle of a flat, dull space. The heat with which she saw him has not been replicated. On one of the images Schnabel has superimposed a big white question mark.

This reproduction is attached to a review of a Schnabel exhibition in France. There's no title to the work, no name identifying Annika. That's all there is. The painting. The woman and her aging beauty. Art took her a certain number of miles and stranded her there.

AN EXTRAORDINARY LIFE

A LOT OF LIFE IS RANDOM. But you can tilt the odds by placing yourself in those situations where good random things are known to occur. Of course randomness works the other way too. The first day of graduate school our painting professor was Tony Smith.

A tall bearded man my father's age, stepping into the studio to confront the cautious, nervous ambitions and brazen insecurities of twelve graduate students. He was wooly-headed and brilliant.

I was twenty-seven, and brilliance seemed to me a manageable phenomenon—like hurricanes or measles, events that could also be handled with sensible precautions. The key attribute was staying power. Get inside the brilliant person's zone of influence, then keep the transmission lines open.

Brilliant people I'd met often seemed focused on interesting things not quite in the room. Then you could see them too. But only after the brilliant people had pointed them out and spoken about them.

This was what brilliant people were for. The risk you didn't take into account was the person at the other end of the transmission, with ambitions and insecurities of their own.

And, of course, Tony was brilliant whether any of us were in the room or not.

So as the semester progressed, what Tony wanted from me became one of those questions that illuminates everything but can't really be faced, like the sun. My own husband was spoiled in the way of attractive people. Half the time he seemed present, solidly there. And then he'd look up at me only as a surprising interruption, a mechanism that either was or wasn't functioning. But even when I was painting in class I could feel the weight of Tony Smith's attention between my neck and shoulders. When he turned away, I'd raise my hand with a question and could feel the extra second he spent disentangling his gaze.

MY BEST FRIEND was a willowy and unwholesomely rich Harvard graduate named Aurelia Kleinman. "What's his age again?" she asked. Her accent—lightly imperious—made you think of the Fitzgerald line about the voice being full of money. We were picking up our children from nursery school. I told her what a sharp dresser Tony was—always in a business suit, when other people weren't arriving in suits that much to Hunter College. "What's his body like?" Orrie asked with a small giggle.

She sipped coffee as we braced ourselves for the door. That interesting moment, all the children pouring through, when we'd instantly stop being adult friends and become all mother. Orrie and I were the only parents wearing sunglasses.

She said quickly, as the knob began to turn, "Fifty-one is a dangerous age, for a man. They get paranoid that you're the last beautiful girl they're ever going to interest. Dangerous for my father. And so, of course, *very* dangerous for my mother." (What Orrie actually said was *mummy*, but I can't bear to write it.) Then Orrie was dropping to one knee for her sons. "Oh, hel*lo* to you, hello to *you!*" I found the alert, worried faces of my own two boys inside the pack. It was heartbreaking the way their faces looked when they didn't spot you immediately.

Orrie was staring at me over her sunglasses. "So tread lightly," she said meaningfully. "I'm just giving Pat hiking advice," she explained to her boys.

Her family was from North Carolina—they'd been rich through all but the first six presidencies. When she talked, you pictured estate forests, private runways, gold keys turning safe-deposit boxes, and politely abandoned plans in astonishing settings. But you could never ask Orrie directly about any of this. It would be rude: you could let her say it, but the data had to come from her, or the implication was that you were making her feel freaky. But every so often she'd lift those light imperious eyebrows and say, "Family event." Then she'd disappear for a few days and come back another person, either reckless-tongued or very good-daughterish in a way that must have reflected the tensions of her growing-up self.

With Orrie, art felt like my private, mysterious thing. A special world to which my own background, plus talent and experience, entitled me. It was my estate. Art can do this, put you on an equal footing.

Life outside Hunter was solid, a sort of square. At breakfast and dinner I was one of four around a table: my husband, me, two children. But during the day there were the twelve of us in that studio, with its smell of paint and colors on canvas and old hissing radiators, being trained for our insane gamble. To become, if we could be, artists. And there was Tony, lordly and slightly ominous, his eyes pinned on me, which seemed an advantage.

EVEN IF YOU don't recognize the name—a hard, direct name that's so much like him—you know his work. Tony Smith made the big black tetrahedron snake sculptures you often find on college campuses or see business people eating in the shade of, ties and scarves whipped by the breeze. A great one prowls the grounds around the National Gallery.

He wasn't famous that way yet. It was all of our luck, Tony being at Hunter Graduate School. And it was my luck—good or bad—that he took this particular interest in me.

People shared rumors. Tony and female grad students; Tony not treating his marriage as any sort of map or limit to behavior. (The fact of Tony's wife didn't mean very much. One item of creepy gossip was about Mrs. Smith driving him to assignations. You could imagine her soft profile at the wheel, waiting outside a dark one-story house.) You'd forget this when you looked at him in class. And then remember after, when he found you with his large, hard blue eyes.

I had been in my own marriage six years, and come to understand the relationship as a kind of giant machine you rode in and somehow thoughtlessly fed your days to. You hardly even knew you were riding in it, as it chewed up days and months. Except for the moments when the machine suddenly broke. Even if it was just the smallest bump. And then you were aware of its thoughtless, gigantic power to ruin.

Even if I hadn't been married, I would have been weirded out. Start an affair with a brilliant person, I thought, and this would light a fuse. The situation could explode in either of two directions. Either the affair would stop—and then no more brilliance, just avoidance and bad feelings. Or, and this was unlikely, if it progressed to marriage you'd end up being, simply, another version of the wife. You'd never really have been a fellow artist at all. In both cases, the brilliance you were there for would stop.

So if you really wanted to paint, the possibility of an affair was like a candle you had to keep lit but with only the tiniest possible flame, one that wouldn't really melt any of the wax.

My friend Orrie had warned me about this. "Men are very, very sensitive mammals. They can be startled and wounded and frightened away by the tiniest movements."

I always asked Tony questions—planned all week—when the class met on Wednesdays. Then he suggested we meet once a week after class, for private discussions, artist to protégé. These were thrilling. We talked as we broke down our painting stations, running hot water through our brushes—the paint giving in sudden delicious, sludgy clumps—and stowed away my canvases. And when we walked outside along the sidewalk crowds and rush hour car horns and smells, through the slanting light and shadows of Lexington Avenue, feeling the city cool into winter along our arms and on our faces and hands, Tony raised his voice to be heard above the soliloquy of traffic.

ANOTHER THING ABOUT brilliant people: they make the rare and elevated feel casual, near. Tony had studied at the Bauhaus—the famous German school so committed to the avant-garde that its faculty had to run from the Nazis. (They reconstituted in Chicago, where Tony met them.) Then he'd spent years as Frank Lloyd Wright's apprentice. Often Tony talked about Jackson Pollock as if he'd just stepped out of the room. Tony had been there at the beginning and end. He'd walked into the Art Students League and met Pollock, then helped lift the coffin as a pallbearer at Pollock's funeral. It put you, mentally, on a first-name basis with art and history. Because you knew someone who had walked through those rooms—Pollock's studio in East Hampton, the Chicago Bauhaus—it felt, by extension, that you'd been there too. That some of that dust had landed on your own shoulders.

When you start, art is limited to the narrowness of what you've been and things you've managed to see. There was a young person's limit to what I'd experienced myself. I was painting what seemed meaningful to me: my two children, in their beds or under the tree shadows in Central Park. At Tony's request, I brought these to class.

It was thrilling to have Tony look at your work: the very active, restless way brilliant people have of taking in material, galloping ahead, and enthusing about it. You can never quite be sure anything you've done really merits such attention. Tony asked, "Can I take some of these home to New Jersey with me? I want to look more." No other painting teacher of mine had ever asked that.

He supplied the best definition of nonrepresentational art I'd ever heard. He demystified it. Tony was very close with the painter Mark Rothko. Rothko's studio was just across the street, the fourth floor of East Sixty-Ninth Street; Tony often came to our class straight from having a look at Mark's work. This often snowed us. To be a block away from all that. He told me, with a frown, that painting true objects from real life was fine. It was all well and good. Painting my feelings for my children was fine. "But the only way to really express true feeling is through abstraction."

It took me a second: the words "express" and "feeling" came from that nervous world of concepts I wanted to exclude when talking with Tony. It took a second for me to make sure he didn't mean them the way I didn't want him to.

"What you're giving me here," he continued, "is an illustration of feeling. But not the feelings themselves." He nodded as if he'd just overheard and liked the way he'd framed the idea. He nodded again. "Only abstraction can give you direct experience of actual emotion, which is what Mark's paintings show us."

To know he'd come from looking at Rothko's paintings to looking at yours: that was the power of a person like Tony. You know they've stood in extraordinary rooms. And if they can like and accept you, somehow it seems as if your work can withstand those rooms as well. You've survived the toughest eyes. Tony explained that the reverse was true. "At my New Jersey place," he said, "we have all kinds of old farm utensils. Tools, supplies, knickknacks, and what have you in the garage. Some of those, you know—you strip off the context, and they could be seen as abstract, beautiful." He looked at me. And here I knew. He was talking about his house with me as a kind of flirt. Because it powerfully excited him—to have the concepts of me and the house joined in his mouth like that.

Sometimes his speech could be a blizzard of first names. Mark. Also Barney—for Barnett Newman, a famous painter, maybe even more famous as a theorist. Jackson was Pollock, who had started everything. Even "Tennessee." For another friend of his, Tennessee Williams. He must have known how these constellations in his daily talk could snow any person in her twenties.

He was a wild anthology of Pollock stories. There he was, talking about the person who had made American art something big and major: glamour is a part of brilliance too. Can you be attracted to somebody you don't find, somehow, glamorous? And for the person on the other end, can you hold the attention of someone whose tastes have been no doubt elevated by constant exposure to the best? Tony was friends with the man who had made American painting, finally, international. He told me, with excitement and regret, about the church he and Jackson once designed together, which somehow never got built. Jackson had refused the commission unless Tony's work was also included. His best story was about that Pollock canvas called *Blue Poles*. The painting became very important, and a point of contention.

Tony, Barney Newman, and Pollock were in Jackson's studio: this was the barn in Springs, East Hampton, down a winding road with a view of the marshes. Jackson was in a low mood. They'd all been drinking, the painting Jackson had on the floor was refusing to come out. As they drank, the three men started putting stuff on it. Then they were all painting on it. First with brushes and sticks, then pressing their fingers and palms into the surface. It became a bacchanal. There was some bleeding; they took off shoes and started walking on it. (The blood was from Newman's foot; he'd nicked his sole on a Coke bottle.) Then Barney got an idea—drawing eight long blue lines, to pull the picture together, and he painted them on. *Blue Poles* eventually sold to the National Gallery of Australia. The highest price then paid for a twentieth-century American canvas.

Lee Krasner, Jackson's widow, disputed the story. This made a rupture between Tony and Lee. So later Tony retracted the whole story. In the cleaned-up version, Jackson had simply been "in a bad way." That was all. When everybody was older, Tony's wife attended the Lee Krasner retrospective at the Whitney. Tony sent her in alone; he didn't want to face Lee. (This time, it was Tony waiting out in the car.) When Lee saw her, she reached out—and then, maybe remembering the *Blue Poles* story, Lee retracted her welcoming arms.

But what you also took away from these stories was daily and nourishing. That it was real people with real and messy lives that art came from. People who made egotistical arguments and had bad habits and spouses and children, all of which I had too.

ORRIE WAS ALWAYS ASKING. Until my stories about Tony became like his about Jackson Pollock. Lots of "Tony said," "Tony did." And Orrie seemed to enjoy putting me in this position: revealing to me all the pleasures I already took from the relationship. There's a sadism in certain kinds of friendships. A forceful showing to you of yourself, or the friend somehow enlisting you in a private argument about their own past, that all people everywhere are disappointing in the same limited number of ways. Orrie advised me to tell my husband about Tony—a connection this big was bound to come out anyway, and I couldn't afford my husband becoming jealous of my work in any way. Trust her. It would become after that a choice of work or family; nobody wants that. "Because either choice is a money-loser," she said in her light voice. "A write-off."

I thought for a moment about Orrie saying "can't afford"—what could that phrase possibly mean to her?

Then Orrie was called away on one of her family functions. This one lasted a week, a great convocation of Gwinnetts, for a discussion of the museums and foundations that the family oversaw, plus the disposition of various mammoth properties. She came back in a vivid, dangerous mood.

I told her the advice about talking Tony over with my husband had been smart. It had woken him up a tiny bit. Also removed some of my guilt: if anything, by making him manageable for my husband too, it had diminished Tony.

She kind of shrugged angrily. We were walking down Sixty-Fifth Street to the nursery school.

"What did it matter, what my husband thought?" she asked.

"What do you mean?" I asked.

I wasn't going to stay with him: "Didn't I see that yet?" She asked this furiously. I told her about his good qualities. How good he was with our boys. How he never got in the way of my painting. How I liked his body, his hair. I wondered why she'd suddenly gone ballistic about my husband and our marriage. Maybe her family visit had put Orrie in a bad mood?

"He's an airport," Orrie said. "Who looks at an airport?" she asked. "Who bothers to really notice an airport," she went on. "An airport is just the place that you leave."

I got what she was saying but was surprised by her angry delivery, which put me off. We rounded a corner into a slash of February lemon sunlight. I thought you could possibly get this by mixing some of the color Aurelian with a touch of Payne's Grey. Orrie pushed up her dark glasses. "You know why I've never done anything? Anything real? I'm talented too." She waved her hand across her torso. "Anything like what you are doing?" And looked down. "No one in my family is allowed to fail. To try their hand and not succeed. Failure is so embarrassing and ordinary." Now she was even walking angrily. Little jabs of her feet, which on a body like hers was a bit ridiculous. There'd been an English professor at school: slightly older and very attractive. He'd thought she had real talent, writing talent. He'd given her reading lists, talked about the famous writers he either knew or exaggerating knowing. They'd become involved. He'd proposed—and here, her family had stepped in. All those Gwinnetts with their heavy foundations and worldliness, who made the alliance impossible. "It's up to you," they told her only when they were certain what her selection would be. Orrie stood firm, then relented. And she told me what the professor said, in his sad university office, when she told him no: "We could have had an extraordinary life."

Tony's life was turning extraordinary. Right around the time I graduated from Hunter he suddenly became famous.

There Tony was, on the cover of *Time* magazine, being called one of America's most talented new sculptors—his was the fastest rise in the New York art world of the late sixties—that demanding, bearded face. He now belonged to the art world, as I read *Time* over breakfast. "The darling of the critics, the envy of every museum collector." Us students had been right, and we'd lost him.

Tony didn't make a big deal about it—but what could it have been for him to walk by a newsstand on the way to our class and see his picture on a row of covers? Like a mirror reflection in the window. It was only for seven days, till the next cover of the magazine: but for those seven days he must have felt more alive.

AND AT THE END OF that week's session, when we were cleaning our brushes, I stayed a little later. Tony turned the water off. It made a kind of extra squirting sound as the flow ended. "There's something I need to say." Some of the water had fanned across his cuffs, which took my eye for a second: that blue suit with water darkening the edge.

He must have been waiting—and with the positive change in one area of his life he wanted to now approach the other. "I've loved you since I first saw you," Tony said. He looked relieved. Then he said an odd thing, for all the declarations of love I've had, seen, and read about. It showed how cool he was in a way to add this—simply because it was, for him, true. "You remind me of my mother."

He waited for me—and when I didn't speak for a while, he waved his hand in the air. "You don't have to say anything now," he said. "I said what I needed to."

AND A FEW WEEKS LATER, I had Tony to dinner. This was his idea. He said he couldn't get me out of his head. I'd avoided Orrie since she'd compared my husband to a departure gate. But I still had to go to school for my children. And the day Tony was to visit, I saw her head with its stylish short haircut at the beginning of the line of mothers. She kept turning over her shoulder—then came and found me.

This was the good daughter version of her: She was now nearly furious with concern. "You have to be ruthless to be happy," she said. "You can be nice and well-meaning and you end up just in the middle. Medium happy, okay happy." She waved her hand around us: at the parents, the school. All consigned by Orrie to okay-ness. Her own husband, Henry Kleinman, was just another Harvard banker. His being

Jewish had been an indulgence and was as far down the scale as her family went. Hard negotiators, they had probably seen it as an acceptable compromise.

"What makes you think you can expect something extraordinary," she said, " if you're only ever willing to act like everybody else?"

TONY CAME TO our apartment with a large wrapped present, set it by the closet door, solemnly shook hands with my husband, rested his hand on his kneecaps as he bent to say hello to my children. He had only ever seen them in paintings. He made the house feel suddenly small—filled it in a way we didn't seem to. We all were attendant on him. And I didn't know why he had wanted to come and the whole thing appeared somehow terribly dangerous: to compare himself with my husband, to claim me, take me from him? Or maybe, just to become more intimate?

I felt the strangeness. Having brought him, with my own young powers, to my house, from his world into mine. And knowing—he and I the only people in the room knowing this—that I could have him at the center of my life if I wanted. That everyone in the room was hanging on his offer. Maybe his bringing himself here was his way of making an offer.

And from the ricketiness of that perch we all sat down. I couldn't hear anything that was said, though I know I nodded and smiled, some social part of me continuing to conduct necessary business as I saw the two men in their places at the table: the square was just the three of us now. And at that moment, I didn't know what I'd do. Tony had told us how important hanging a show was: a painting could look great by itself but then not as good when you hung it next to the wrong canvas for an exhibition. Everything was context. When I started my own showing, and I still remembered many things Tony had said, I understood how right he was, and how generous it had been, at this pitched moment, for him to think to share it. And Tony for a moment did look every year of his age, across from my young, handsome husband. My husband looked smooth. Then my eyes adjusted, and I could see again how extraordinary he was. Tony asked if we had anything to drink, preferably scotch. My feelings were shifting by the second.

And from that situation—one of those moments when anything might happen—Tony proceeded to get unbelievably, impossibly drunk. He became as drunk as I'd ever seen anybody drunk. Drunk in the way of the past's drunks. Of the people for whom drunkenness was a truer state, interrupted by wasteful periods of sobriety.

And then drunk in a strangely unappealing way: as time passed all the alcohol seemed to consolidate in his nose. After about an hour, the bridge of his nose would wriggle and squinch up and down like a rabbit's. He drank for two solid hours: he sang a song about being Irish, and then one about a grasshopper but most of the second verse was mushed. Eventually, my husband lifted his eyebrows at me and relaxed into nonobservance: it was as if, earlier, some essential part of him had sensed a danger to himself, a threat to his settled life, and now that objective cold self sensed that the danger had passed. He nodded at me. One more bit of irony: marriage had allowed my husband to join a long line, to partake in a great cultural observance. We'd both joined a line that extended to Mark Rothko and Jackson Pollock and perhaps even Frank Lloyd Wright and many others: people who had gotten to see Tony Smith drunk. I'd heard about but never experienced his drunkenness—for me it was the cutoff point.

My husband excused himself, rose from the table at ten o'clock to check on the boys. I whispered to Tony, asking if he was all right. We were alone at the table, and I wanted to see what he would say. My moment of decision had passed. This was a life I did not want. His nose went through another unbelievable series of twitches. "Sure," he said. Then he rested his cheek on his dessert plate as if it were a pillow.

When I asked how he was getting back to New Jersey, he said he'd need a cab. I couldn't imagine how he could hail one. I pictured the many hurdles between our table and the passenger seat. He'd have to first navigate the hallway. Then pilot the many-buttoned, suddenly elaborate cockpit of the elevator. Cross the desert of our lobby. And then face the unpredictable freelance personnel of the street. There was quite an adventure in front of him. I understood I was responsible for getting him home. As we went through the door, he grabbed the gift he'd brought. He lurched upright.

In the lobby Tony said, "It's all okay, all okay." I agreed. It was okay. Then at the door he gave me his gift again, the brown paper–wrapped square. "For you," he said. "Real things, they can be abstract too," he said.

Outside on the street I hailed and seated him in the cab. And felt relieved he was leaving.

As my husband watched TV in the bedroom, I removed the brown twine and paper from around Tony's gift. It was, as he'd told me, the industrial farm stuff from his home in the country. A burlap sack, with framing nails tacking it against a light wood stretcher bar. Purina Hen Chow, it said. It was beautiful. From the industrial stuff, the barn stuff from his home in the country. And how brilliant of Tony to see the art there.

He'd connected the concept of his house and me again, in this visceral way.

My children especially loved it: and their loving it was always a kind of secret between who I now was and who I'd been then, the circumstances of the gift. When I had my first show a year later, becoming successful so fast that Tony's face and my face were advertised together in *Art Forum,* on separate pages, so if you closed them the faces were together. And when I opened it again, he looked as remote and glowering as he had that first day of class. As if he'd never been somebody who had given me anything personal. This was the treasure I held off selling until the bitter end, when everything had changed again. And when I brought it to Sotheby's, since Tony had never signed it, I was told the piece was simply without value. There was no way to prove the brilliance was his or if it was mine.

SEVEN WORDS

TONY SMITH ONCE told me a great thing. About scheduling. He explained that if he wanted to go somewhere, or do something with Jackson Pollock in East Hampton, he'd just get on the phone, call him up, and same day Jackson would be there.

"Sure, Tony," Jackson would say. In Tony's imitation, Jackson had a different voice than you'd expect: higher and more sensitive. Unlike the paintings, full of that thrashing confidence, "What time should we meet?"

Tony would say, "In two hours."

And just like that, whatever time it was, there Jackson would be. Dungarees, cigarette, paint under his fingernails. Tony told us what the real ID for painters was. Your hands would never again be quite clean.

There was none of the prima donna stuff you associate with artists. The sensitive preparation, the uninterruptable rituals of concentration, the vow and holy orders of working. Just, "Okay—what time do we meet?"

From the artist everybody deep down wanted to be. Whose impact had exploded across so many painters' studios and ambitions. The name young artists aspired to. So you could say the name and everyone understood the aspiration. He loved paint, and he loved fun. And when painting Jackson had so much control, Tony explained, he could adapt himself to the allotted time, paint what he had to in two hours, finish when the clock said he had to. Art shouldn't be sacred. So I patterned myself on that. It was a good discipline. You had to take yourself seriously. But then stop at the seductive point where you treated your own whims and techniques as iron and holy. If I only had two hours to paint, that was fine—I adjusted. I sometimes think those seven words have to be the goal. To do the work as naturally as anything else—cleaning the kitchen or opening a book or taking a walk. I'd think of it, those seven words, as a motto for working on something with such a steep drop: as art into the other parts of life. To make the drop less steep. *Okay, when do you want to meet?*

A couple years later when I got to know Jackson's widow, Lee Krasner, she said Tony had it completely wrong. She had invited me to the old house on Springs Fireplace Road. Which had the rich, salt-drenched smell of nearby water, harsh and soft at the same time. Above that the sweet smell of lawn with a lot of moist-petaled wildflowers growing in it. Lee walked me around the sudden alleys of lawn that made up the property: the ground felt strangely pliable too. It did not feel like the chaotic, stormy place where American art was finally born.

My dealer's second—I was at perhaps the best gallery in the city—had given me Lee's phone number. I was selling two or three paintings every week. I had not been prepared for the effect this would have on former teachers, and am happy to pass along this warning to students everywhere. Your professors are ready to like you, and will like you forever, so long as the relationship does not turn. They are encouraging only until you are on some kind of shared footing. Past that they can be competitive and even hostile creatures who want the things you have and do not want to acknowledge it and do not want you to share what they have.

I thought maybe I was imagining this, but then I ran into one of these professors at a museum. He was actually moving away from me, at speed. Vincent Longo, with his sad goatee. He said, "Not me, Pat—but lots of faculty at Hunter are angry at you." And when I caught up with him, under a big French painting by the stairs of a scientist and his wife, he repeated, "It's not me. But there's a lot of people who are very angry."

Lee wasn't angry. She wore a blue checked dress that looked like a tablecloth and also very housewifely. Unlike Tony Smith, she never called her dead husband Jackson. Always Pollock. She didn't have to make a point of it. She had shared his bed. She had the kind of fierce homeliness—protruding lips, large powerful nose—so unrepentant it can power itself into a variety of beauty. *Jolie-Laide*, the French call it.

EVERYONE WHO'D KNOWN HER had a story about her. The person I have been the most impressed by in my life, said that she, Lee, was the most formidable person he'd ever known. The story that I liked best was about her psychotherapy. Lee quit analysis. She felt she'd extracted what there was to extract. But by then the therapist had become so dependent on her that he phoned Lee every day.

After I'd been there in that soft marshy air for a few hours, with flies coming out as the sun softened and the air went gray with the damp feel you get beside the water, as if small rain clouds are massing, a tall man named Harold Rosenberg came by. He was very tall and mustached, the art critic for the *New Yorker*. With one of those shiny faces like a slab of uncooked meat—a face that a certain kind of New York life produced. Sloppy and forceful. The scene was a young person's vision of the artist life: of course you have iced tea with Jackson Pollock's widow, Lee Krasner, who brings you glass after glass of iced tea, and of course the *New Yorker*'s art critic just drops by. Rosenberg had sacked out on the rickety outdoor sofa Lee kept on her porch. I had been in school only a few semesters before. And for all I knew her life really was like this. Rosenberg had been a friend of hers since the late thirties. And lived nearby.

When she talked about Pollock it wasn't as Tony had suggested, just meeting at four in the afternoon. His life sounded more scheduled. For instance Lee—his own wife—wasn't allowed to informally walk into his studio. "I had to be invited," she said.

And Pollock would become, like every serious artist, extremely nervous about his work. When he finished one of the first drip paintings, he formally invited Lee into the barn where he painted. Pollock didn't ask her, "Do you think it's a good painting?" What he asked was, "Do you think it's a painting?"

And in the times between paintings, when he worried, again as artists do, he became very restless and performed household repairs and projects on their property. Even these were shaped with anxieties. He built himself special bookshelves that hid his books, with their incriminating titles. He considered somebody knowing what he was actually reading or had read to be too personal. As Lee showed me the shelves, I thought about how much of his personality he'd hidden, the same way, from Tony.

Lee was in her early sixties. A forceful age. But everyone then, more than two decades above my own age, just seemed to fall under the same category: older. And to be coping with the additional years either more or less well. Up to a certain point. In the same way her features were blunt, her talk was blunt: maybe the years of thrusting herself on an art world that resisted her had taught Lee there was no other way to be. You had to use every opportunity you were given—wrest it away. You had to say what you truly felt.

She would not have been able to meet Tony Smith on two hours' notice. When she was working, Lee told me, she treated herself like a gestapo agent, and wouldn't permit herself to do anything for long stretches but paint. She was Jewish, and that was the way she put it— the harshest way. She would paint for days and days. And one day she would set aside everything and go through all the things she'd left undone, she said, like a whirlwind.

We were, my husband and I, packing up to leave the city. I had made my plans without realizing that Tony's stories about Jackson being able to paint whenever were, perhaps, exaggerated. I had made certain plans based on it. I had earned so much money my husband had begun talking, with an increasing panic, about exchanging the city for New

England. If Jackson could work anywhere, the same should also be true of me. What gave me the right to be fancier about myself than Pollock? I didn't think, in the artist's self-preserving way: I am working well here. Let it continue until every bit of ease and goodness from this place has been used and it all dries up.

Lee told me she was tearing up her old work—failed stuff from twenty years before—then pasting it back together as collage on canvas. She had become, I saw, bitter. As we walked through my square apartment on East Eighty-Eighth Street, Lee admitted she did not even have a gallery. Getting a gallery had been so easy for me that I was unsure I had understood properly, or how this could have happened, or why she was revealing it. This was how bad things had gotten. Then that forceful face brightened with shrewdness.

"But there's one thing," she said. "I haven't made a commitment on Pollock's estate." What she meant was which of the major dealers she would allow to handle all of his remaining work. It would be guaranteed money, after all. She told me she intended a deal so that of the four galleries pitching the estate—including Marlborough, and then Pace, one of the two greatest spaces in the city then—she was going to sign only *with the one* that would commit to her work as well. That was what it had come to: it was the only way she could get her pictures shown in New York. And it succeeded. Lee saved herself, that way. So maybe women had to be more resourceful, or Tony hadn't listened that hard, or never said those seven words, or Jackson hadn't ever really been willing to let friends see the titles of his books.

A BAR AT THE
FOLIES BERGÈRE

WITH NO PREAMBLE they appeared in my bedroom: blues and whites and a row of bottles. They were hanging when I came home from school.

The still life with a plaster cupid made the biggest impression. I couldn't get over the sureness with which the painter—at age sixteen I didn't recognize it was Cézanne—had done it. During the years before college I drew that still life many times in my sketchbook.

There were six others. All, to my teenage eye, French, Impressionist, extremely vivid and beautiful. The only person who could've hung the reproductions was my father. And this was his way. He usually operated behind the scenes. I had just come home—Dad knew I wanted to be a painter—and there they were.

We never discussed the reproductions; they simply became part of my bedroom. And then, over the years, the pictures—with their familiar configurations—stayed in my mind.

I still retain, in a part of my chest, the mood it put me in to see these eight images. One I especially liked featured a girl who looked to be about my age. She stood at the center. Her facial expression reminded me of what I believed I was suffering from. Something I couldn't name, but that had become a daily affliction: a sense of nothingness. It was reassuring to find the feeling on another face. There was a sadness too. Also a frankness. I identified with the girl's look of dazed resignation. And sometimes in the morning before school, or at night after finishing homework, I'd stare at her. Had this been all that was available to her? Why did she look so glum? Would this happen to me as well?

The painting contained a man too. He was of less interest. Crucially idealized—collar, mustache, top hat—while the girl was not, was specific and real. My read was that he was possibly her father, demanding his barmaid daughter leave and return to a sensibly ordered home. Later, when I researched the painting, I learned scholars believe him to be a high-end john, or even a roué, making her a slightly unwelcome but—as her expression reveals—not entirely unfamiliar or surprising proposition.

My father had his eyebrows raised at dinner that first night after I had put down my bags and examined the walls. I smiled and nodded at him. That was enough. We never discussed what had given him the idea, where he had bought such lovely, expensive prints. My father preferred that role: the generosity, mystery, and elegance of it was his way. He had a talent for procuring great small valuable things from the outside world. The girl in the painting offered a sense of what it was to be female. My father's grace—doing not just what was needed but a little extra, and never calling attention to his accomplishment: an ideal of effective and unshowy performance—might be a portrait of one aspect of being male.

WE HAD DECIDED to go ahead with the party anyway. It was 1973. I was thirty-one. The day had remained misty—that seaside brume that makes the lungs heavy, turns them salty and clogged. And it was not a mistake; the mist made all of us feel more sealed in, and thus bigger to each other. There seemed to be no one else in the world. Just us and this mist. Artist parties are somehow much more physical than other parties: words are not the forte of people who work all day with canvas and iron, with bolts of fabric, tubs of color, and with minerals and torches. Talk is less delicate, less cushioned.

There we all were, circulating on the damp, shushing, and invisible sand. We had gotten the bonfire started, with the surf's crash and gravel next to us. We couldn't see, but we could sometimes feel, the spray, and always hear the roar. Hands would touch yours as they passed you a drink, a joint, a plate with food on it—and sometimes a finger would inquisitively stroke the inside of a wrist, or a palm would frankly grip your forearm, and you'd look to see a man with that question on his face. I could feel the dampness going down the ankles of my socks, and the side of my body facing the ocean was cold and drenched.

LARRY ZOX—I recognized his truck—had just pulled in down near where our blankets and bottles and fire were. With his high beams up and reflecting weirdly in the fog, with sudden bits of spray filtering through the two cones like lively bugs, he opened his door and windows and turned up his stereo. Dylan sounding a little ominous, in the way that left you freer to act but also slightly nauseated. Overstimulated. The music was license. For artists and sculptors who often didn't need more than a tiny bit of license. Dylan was explaining that by and large, in whatever situation, however you looked at things, everyone really did get stoned.

Some people were congratulating me. I'd had the biggest show of anybody in our group. The most successful show of any young painter for a while. I learned a distinction that night: the better-educated men—the more sensitive men—wanted to congratulate you. And perhaps prize out the secret of how you'd pulled something like that off: Did you know someone at the newspapers, an influential critic, or someone at art journals? Were dealers nicer to you? How did the whole thing feel, to have gotten the thing everyone talked about? Who were your collectors? Were there museum curators flocking once everyone saw there was money to be made? This last seemed a deliberately callous way to put it, to show they weren't afraid. They could get the assurance they needed. Perhaps, by treating you, once they mastered their fear, with a little bit of dismissiveness. The more insensitive of the male artists just wanted to fuck you. To possess your bit of success, and thus overcome it, master it in *that* way? I might have just sold seventy paintings, but their faces said if they could fuck me, that would mean they'd emerge from the experience the bigger of us two.

After some hours the mix became too rich. I walked away from the loud knot we'd made on the edge of the water, farther from the headlights of Zox's truck. The talk and the crowd seemed surprisingly small at a distance. Robert Allen Zimmerman of Hibbing, Minnesota, was explaining behind me, far below, how everyone, eventually, *had* to get stoned. As I got farther still, and could hear even more clearly the shushing of my sneakers on the sand, he had moved on to describing "all-night girls . . . whispering of escapades out on the 'D' train." That was the miracle of art. He'd seen it once, or thought it, arranged it, and now it was available for everyone. It was not a small thing.

Our ostensible host was a distant cousin of the first lady of a glamourous and recently assassinated president. Her beach mansion was a half mile from our party. I smelled sea grass—its green and pleasing sourness—and chilly sea air. Then I was beyond the dunes and walking along the red-painted and rusty-wired picket fence, and down much softer sand toward Anne's great big haunted-looking pile of a house. A looming shape, gray in this light. It was past nine. Her side door was open, and the house felt eerie and cool and solid after swimming in the foggy humanness of the party. Caterers were walking back and forth in the kitchen emptying trays.

I walked into her living room. I was becoming less drunk. I was a newly separated woman alone in a big house. In the library, I dropped down into a large wing chair. This room was all oak and leather with a heavy, old, expensive Kerman Persian carpet in the middle, plus dark fixtures that felt nineteenth century. I shivered a little. Far off I could still hear Bob Dylan, but not what he was singing about. It felt mature, to have what I had wanted, and also to be able to have had *enough* of it. To not need to greedily stay. I reached for a book on the table. An oversize Harry Abrams book: *Manet*, very deluxe. I fanned through its big pages at random. A little breeze came up from them. I turned to a picture of a woman at a bar, a young woman, now much younger than I was. The painting my father had hung, with seven others, on my walls that day when I was a girl.

I had looked at it so long, so many nights, that a part of me was still stuck to it. It's the same feeling you get when you find a book you loved, in the edition you loved it in, on a stranger's bookcase: How did that piece of you make its way there? A truer you, as earlier images of you so often are.

It also seemed to be a message from my father, and even from my younger self. A hello, and a reminder. We are you too.

THIS BRITISH PAINTER John Livingston, who I'd bumped into a few times at gallery openings in New York that spring, had invited me to stay in his London loft. At that moment I was grateful to John. He was going to be the deus ex machina extracting me from a bad situation, conveying me through an excruciating transition. From being my sons' mother and caretaker to not being anyone's mother.

During the planning phase conducted by blue air-mail letters, there was one thing he neglected to mention—his marriage. Which meant his London loft would include a wife. Only when we were walking toward his car in Heathrow Airport's parking lot did he broach that topic.

"Oh and by the way. Something I forgot to mention."

"What's that?"

"Not the biggest deal, really. Just thought you might like to know. My wife, Mavis—I'm married, you see—is sitting right in visitor parking in our car." He pointed. Something must have gone wrong with plans—maybe she'd canceled a trip. He had looked so uncomfortable at the gate, and now I understood why.

Sure enough I could see a woman in the car, sitting in John's back seat, leaving me the legroom. Under the circumstances, very considerate. Early fifties, face and body widening—with the sense of giving in to it, letting whatever time wanted to do to her happen, which ambitious people mostly don't go for in New York. Age and fat are to be fought, like traffic: youth, to the last unwrinkled square inch, is to be held on to like a favorable lease. "Mavis, Pat. The artist visiting from New York. Pat, Mavis."

Some people are good at surprises. I am not. I was more or less speechless. It was a very quiet drive to their loft.

They slept below in an open area. I went up the stairs to a loft bed that had the feel of something shipboard. What had they had in mind? What had *John* had in mind? But with the boys leaving and so much else gone, I had grabbed this invitation like a lifeline, without considering what might be expected from me in return. That is, had John expected that drab transaction, the physical tussle, the few moments in sheets in a quick, guilty room, for housing? Why would such a thing even be appealing? Had he—I pondered this with my head a few feet from their ceiling, on the loft bed twelve feet above their floor—expected some kind of ménage?

And still—and this is the thing—I was grateful to be there. Still it was preferable to being in New York. This was how rickety things had become. My thought was not *How dare they?* But *Will I have to leave?* We can fall and fall, as people. And fall again. Better being in London than America.

IN THE INTERVENING four years my life had become a shambles. I'd lost almost everything. And as a result of other people's whims, and bad advice, I was now in London like a displaced person. In a very ugly final divorce, since the successful party at Anne's, my former husband, like Rumpelstiltskin, had come back to get not one, but two children. He'd convinced both sons and the female judge, who was smitten with him, to allow J. to take the two children to that cultural mecca, Mexico, to live with him and their new stepmother. Thereby attempting to erase me. The boys and I had just spent the summer together while he packed up. Hence, John.

MAVIS WAS DOWNSTAIRS cooking the next morning. And the smell was everywhere: grilled tomatoes, eggs, roasted potatoes, and bread, all in the same skillet.

I wheeled my stuff to a cab stand. Money was a concern too, but when you wake in a bad situation, you often wake to what is called self-respect. I think this really is protecting your future memory of a situation: what you want to be preserved in your own mind as what you were capable of accepting. As well as that, by morning, the idea of staying with both of them was simply untenable. When I told John I was leaving, there was a look on his face that seemed somehow familiar, and I have no idea what expression my own face had settled into. I just wanted the exchange to take up as little time as possible. Wheeling my luggage outside on that slightly sunny morning, in September 1977, felt vaguely like a liberation. I had gotten out and now found myself driving through the quiet Bloomsbury section of London. I asked the driver to stop when I saw a phone booth and called to reserve a room. The bellboy took my bag, and we climbed up the stairs to my third-floor room. The walls had no paintings of any kind, just lightly gray in the morning light. Then I unpacked, and sat in that shabby room.

I'd been married and divorced. My ex-husband had taken my sons. Had they been daughters it might not have been as easy. But they were prepubescent—the age when boys seem to need their fathers. He had remarried and taken my two beautiful children to Mexico. The ache of it had been nearly impossible. Ex-husbands do all kinds of horrible things to ex-wives—a long freeway of taunts and revealed disloyalties and fights about money—but generally stop at the red light of taking their children.

I hadn't seen my sons in months. My father had died while they were in Mexico. Then, finally, the boys had visited with me—my children, "visiting"—from May until the middle of August.

WITHIN FORTY-EIGHT HOURS I had a sort of routine in London. It was a single woman's routine. I'd wake, run three miles, bathe, consume a huge English breakfast in the hotel's run-down communal dining hall, then wander the city. The English faces, the men and women, different in their way from American faces, flicked by me like slides projected very fast in an art history lecture. I would find a museum to look into, then be back in my monastic room by seven to read, eat English sandwiches, and fall asleep at ten. Three days passed this way.

That August, the boys had flown west to Los Angeles on a Monday, and I had packed up our summer house by the beach and driven myself to the airport forty-eight hours later for the flight to London. The divorce had been devastating in a way the separation had not been. It had destroyed everything in its wake: my loft, my family, my art dealer connection. How could someone morph into this kind of a monster? Or maybe he'd been that monster all along and I just hadn't noticed. Nine years of seeing my ex-husband every day, sleeping together every night, confiding in him, knowing the sounds he made in the bathroom. Bearing him two children. And all that time unable to identify him as my enemy. How could I have been that naive? Or was it just plain stupid?

I CRIED SOMETIMES when I walked, when the afternoon backlit the thick plane trees behind the park's spiked, iron fences. Little streaky, quiet tears, in this city where nobody knew who I was.

The museum I walked into was called the Courtauld Gallery. I'd never heard of it. It was a strange British name, stuffy-sounding. I imagined it might be a sort of historical society, with floor-to-ceiling bookshelves and a heavy library like Anne's by the ocean and interesting but ultimately full of dull stories about the careers of its founders.

But it turned out to be a good, solid museum. And there was the consolation that art always offers. Art can take me above almost anything. It replaces whatever you've recently made of your life with the best of what other people can do. When you are an artist, you join a culture-spanning religion, and the part of you that is impersonal, that is an artist, can be reabsorbed into the stream of art where you encounter the trickle. It will lift you above the incidents of the personal. Know Rembrandt from the Lowlands, the Chola Bronzes from a much more ancient version of India—know them, learn them, and you will be rescued from the shores of the personal and returned into that stream of culture. And if you produce good enough work, you can join the current of that stream.

As I walked through the gallery, I felt myself recognizing some of the paintings. In this museum with the stuffy name I'd never before heard. There was a Monet whose shape I seemed to know very well: a cloudy path leading up to a garden. Around the next corner there was a small blue-and-white Cézanne still life, with a chalky white Cupid bust in the middle. I was also very surprised to turn a corner and see the girl from the painting I'd studied so many mornings in my home. Still in front of her on a light gray marble slab were the bottles, the flowers in a vase, and tangerines in a glass bowl.

I sat down on one of those plush maroon cushioned visitors' couches across from it. My father's presence was strong with me: the way he smelled, the loose, tan corduroy jacket he always wore. In my chest I could feel my old house. It was warmth trickling back into my head. And I gazed at the face of the barmaid, looking out with that look of hers—acceptance and resilience. The face saying, "Yes, yes, I am strong and not surprised." The beautiful face without even a hint of boredom.

Someone had bought the prints from the Courtauld in London, and my father had found the portfolio in a New York shop. I remembered him—his grace, love of family, the love and confidence he had for me. Had he lived another year, I could have told him about this afternoon at the Courtauld. But now everything was simply with me. To store, carry, and remember.

SEEING THE PICTURE reminded me of the years before the marriage that had just undone me. When, as a teenager, I'd study *A Bar at the Folies Bergère* in my bedroom—and end up mostly looking at the girl's face, which seemed so much like mine. And I remembered who I had been then, and also who I was now.

COMP. LIT.

TO BE A YOUNG WOMAN in Brooklyn in 1958 was to know, as one of the last generations to possess this queasy, bracing knowledge, that the gender facts weren't in your favor. Neither were the religious ones. We got the news that the Ivy League colleges had quotas—anything beyond a certain helping of Jews would quite spoil the taste of the dish the schools were simmering. There were eight good colleges that could take you out of Brooklyn. The ones designed for girls—Smith, Bryn Mawr—had a croquet-mallet and summer-dress flavor. You somehow didn't associate them with the subway at rush hour. Then there was Radcliffe, for the valedictorian alone. And Cornell, which had just begun admitting girls, and had an unbelievable 10:1 male-to-female-student ratio. You had to conduct high school as a campaign. You had to be more or less willing to murder for a 96 grade point average. Somehow I managed to pull that off, accompanied by a portfolio of paintings.

And that's how I came to be sitting in a lecture hall at Cornell University. Which I loved. I'm not sure I've ever loved a single place more. It could look misty and lumpy. The college was surrounded by gorges—deep drops whose gravity the occasional unhappy student would test, about one every two years, with sad and successful results. Colleges seem to exist outside time: my high school felt like the fifties but Cornell just felt like college, like being young. There was a joke about Cornell weather. We got only two seasons: winter and mud. Winter was one long, endless white dumping of snow; spring was the snowmelt. There were famous professors. Arthur Mizener, who'd written the first book about F. Scott Fitzgerald and so everywhere he went trailed a shimmer of Paris—zinc bars and sleepless, smoky parties and Hemingway and Fitzgerald shadowboxing each other for their careers. Vladimir Nabokov had just published *Lolita* and—a bit of an insult—closed up his and his wife's house and put Cornell behind him forever. The professors glazed the landscape with celebrity, and you felt lucky for seeing them outside of class, munching on a lettuce-and-cottage-cheese salad in Goldwyn Smith Hall.

Just being away from home felt lucky, felt glamorous too. (*Glamour* is good luck other people know about.) Freed from family muck, from stuck old patterns, freed from everything. I'd been the only child in my house: all the hopes, ambition, attention, and troubles focused on me. Here, you could make believe you were someone new, which is the lift college gives you and I think one of the things people miss when they miss being in college. Being recruited in an army of learning, your specific history erased to just your name and abilities. Seeing other people at Cornell, in the Uris Library, you'd all at once smile; after a moment they'd smile back. They were having the same lucky experience you were.

I lived my second year on top of a turreted building called Risley Hall. My room was in a tower on its sixth floor. I'd convinced my roommate she didn't really want to spend half her day climbing all those stairs, so I lived alone. In the lobby there was stuffy furniture from upstate New York and a lone apple machine. You put in a quarter and out plopped an apple. I used to buy apples just for the hilarious, pleasant, executioner's suspense—the apple inching forward, rolling, then plummeting. There were dorm mothers—women who looked ready to take care of anything, though not much of anything came up. I liked them: stable, not full of surprises, they were my idea of wholesome. (*Wholesome* was a notion that appealed to my father. He wanted everything in the world to be wholesome, but in his own life this value eluded him.)

TO SIT IN THAT ROOM at Risley, reading a book someone paid to be wiser than me felt might do me some good, next to an open window, and smell the breeze, stirring and cold with a lot of soil in it, was as happy as I'd ever been.

Cornell had accepted me as an art student. In academics I was a grind (academics was a clock-face challenge; if you could log enough hours you could outlast the assignment), but as an art student I was way above average. My senior year I'd won a national painting award, administered by Scholastic. The award included having my photo taken by a Brooklyn newspaper. As my mother drove us downtown, she grew more and more agitated and irritable. My mother's life, we were both aware, contained some lurid elements—she knew firsthand how odd things could get, and she read the newspaper with an intensity and suspicion with which I've never seen anyone read anything. As an overall weather report, scanning for storm fronts and systems that might blow across the city and sock people closest to her. It was the kind of thing that made me happy to be leaving for Cornell. We rolled onto Court Street. My mother pulled the hand brake. She turned to me and asked, "How do we know they're not white slavers?"

The other reason I was at Cornell was to avoid the standard studio-art curriculum. Drawing, painting, composition. All the mechanics, the stuff for pencil and eye. It was good to do, but my brain wanted more. In those years it felt hungry; it had a gravity; it wanted to pull in *more*. Data, chapters, characters. It thumped the table and called out, "More. More." I spent my class time basking outside the studio. Philosophy, anthropology, psychology—what I liked best was anything that sounded scientific, things that ended in that reassuring scientific "-ology." Stuff that was universal and nourishingly impersonal. I wanted to know about all of it. I used to sit in the library with books stacked on my lap, so excited about learning that I didn't know which to open first.

Mostly I studied in McGraw Library, with its nineteenth-century obelisk-like tower and smell of polished wood. During breaks I indulged in another kind of study: Manhattan private high school coeds who sat nearby in their fabulous, understated designer outfits. I'd never seen this kind of clothing before. My idea of chic was Loehmann's.

On the quad I watched the midwestern girls walking back from chapel on Sunday mornings, all wearing circle pins. What did they signify? It didn't matter—I immediately rushed to the campus bookstore and bought one.

There were brilliant ivory-tower professors—all men. Whether specialists in Renaissance lit or *Guernica*, they expressed total devotion to their subjects. Before "diversity" the students were all more or less assimilated and their professors forever on guard against only one thing, the "middlebrow."

SECOND SEMESTER of sophomore year, I came across Proust. So this is a look at how we first met—how I first bumped into his book. It really is like dating, reading. You have your flings. And even when these don't work out, they usefully condition the heart.

What's strange, unnerving, is that I could just as easily *not* have read it. I'd signed up for a course that intrigued me solely because of its name. Comp. Lit. It sounded systematic, abbreviated, beguiling, potentially European. Something to be done with tongs, wearing a lab coat. We'd compare not "books," "novels," not even "literature," but "Lit."

The fourth novel we got was Proust's *Swann's Way*. I can still remember the excitement of the cover. Blue, a man's silhouetted head, laurel wreaths to either side. What could this be about? A path? A bird? An elegant, birdlike man *on* a path? I can still remember the flavor, in Risley, of not knowing, the mystery of what the book might contain. Proust has a section in his first volume about how the names of things—Italian cities, monstrous surfside hotels—strike different resonances in us before we ever experience what it is they do name. Just because of their associations. "[E]ven on a stormy day, the name of Florence or Venice gave me a desire for the sun, for lilies," he writes. "Words present us with little pictures of things, clear and familiar, like those that are hung on the walls of schoolrooms, to give children an example of what is meant by a carpenter's bench, a bird, an ant-hill." He writes, "I need only, to make them reappear, pronounce the names. . . ." That's how it is with a new book. A new book is a new world. And it's fun to refeel that little bit of dizziness in the chest and shoulders, as you circle its runway, before you land and discover what type of world it contains.

I opened the cover and read sentences like this. "In our lives the days are not all equal. To get through each day, natures that are slightly nervous, as mine was, are equipped, like automobiles, with different speeds." This was how a day felt. And Proust wasn't embarrassed by the fact that some natures could be slightly nervous; it was just a fact. "There are mountainous, arduous days, which one spends an infinite time climbing. And downward-sloping days that one can descend at full tilt, singing as one goes."

I'd never read anything like that. A day's complete emotional anthology, along with how our personalities can differ as we travel inside one. It tingled in me—as a real book does—because I seemed to know it already. It was my own experience, but just outside the borders, over the stone wall, of what I could name. And it had warm news in it. That our internal states and shifts mattered enough to deserve their proper description.

It was that pause in the year, the turn between winter and mud. I had a world in my hands. Smelling dirt and frost through the window. And I had Proust, whom I would continue to study most of my life.

LEAD PIPE CINCH

YOU MEET PEOPLE TWICE. The person they want you to meet. And sometime later—to your surprise and disadvantage and their insufficiency—the person they helplessly, endlessly are.

One of the reasons my former husband moved up the ladder in advertising was his inability to feel anything for whomever he was pushing out. People would get fired to clear his path; he noted it, but without emotional content. No families at the kitchen table, late into the night, planning their anxious next moves. I don't mean you would expect him to mourn. We are all, in the world as it is organized, predators. But you would expect him to note it without celebration. The idea had always seemed to be to extract the most one could while causing the least bloodshed to the henhouse all around.

J. was mostly interested in what everything cost. And where you could get the cheapest prices. He went through the motions of living by following what other people did. Even in sex he performed by rote—you do this, then I'll do that, usually in the same order.

When I married him on the rebound from my first serious boyfriend, I hadn't known him very well. As a college friend who'd met him four years before me put it: "I'd been familiar with his sloth and irresponsibility." What neither of us were in on was the violence that ran through his family, almost like a gene, from one generation to the next.

J. HAD LEFT HOOSICK FALLS, the small and depressed upstate New York town we'd moved to a few years before so he could become a writer, and driven straight to his new girlfriend's apartment on the Upper East Side. After that, for appearance's sake he got his own place on East Third Street— the Hells Angels' block. Then, after the shortest time possible, he moved into her apartment permanently.

I was a painter, and my second exhibition was scheduled for that November. It was crucial that it succeed, in the same way that the second book following the bestseller must also sell. There is the secondary, sporting question, under the desire simply to enjoy a book or exhibition. The audience wonders, *Can the painter, or writer, do it a second time?*

In my case there'd been too many changes in too short a period— moving to the country, separating, changing painting styles and mediums (acrylic to oil). What's the difference between the two? Because it is water-based, acrylic paint moves easily. And it can be applied to the support with almost anything: sponges, mops, squeegees. Oil, as in oil-based paint, has, as its binder, linseed oil, and its solvent is not water but mineral spirits. These are thicker substances, so covering a large area of canvas with oil paint will be slower. And it's usually applied with brushes that have to be arduously cleaned after each color. There is one clear advantage to oil paint over acrylic, and that is its brilliance of color. Rule of thumb: when you've had a huge success with one, don't switch. Your audience has just gotten to know where to meet you, and already you are gone.

By then our sons, Jon and David, were nine and seven, barely old enough for camp. The timeline had been: we split up in April, the boys and I left Hoosick Falls in late June, then they went to camp July 1, and I went back to my New York studio to paint. So when J. came, I was alone, and there would be no one to intrude on my aloneness.

Thrilled to be back in Manhattan, I even kneeled down and kissed the pavement. For the first time in my life, I was on my own. Once I stayed in my queen-size studio bed the whole day reading *Portnoy's*

Complaint. During the previous nine years I'd always been on call—to make breakfast, to ready the kids for school or the park, then to make everybody's dinner. That was in addition to attending graduate school in painting. I was thirty years old and tired. When I saw someone who remembered me from those grad school days, years later, she said, "You were always frantic."

THAT SUMMER with the children gone and no husband, all I did was paint, from six in the evening until around two in the morning. Then I'd sleep until noon.

Like a true beginner, I decided to create a new body of work in the two months prior to the show. Even though there were many paintings I'd done during the two years between the first and second exhibitions good enough to hang. It was a classic extreme anxiety response, which meant I'd have to create eight similarly first-rate pictures in two months. Highly unlikely.

The gallery could have been more hands-on too, and told me to calm down. But the art dealer, André Emmerich, wasn't watching that closely, or maybe he'd already been put off by (a) my move to the country, (b) my separation, (c) my new painting style. Maybe he thought I was flaky. Not the biggest problem because if I failed there'd be literally dozens of artists instantly ready to take the spot that had become mine. Having the talent and not making money on it—or not having other people make money on it—is, in the art world, the same thing as not having the talent at all. So much money is at stake with art that there were no quiet successes, only noisy triumphs and absolutely muffled disappearances by failure.

ONE AFTERNOON, unexpectedly, J. arrived at the studio building. The freight elevator didn't work on weekends, but anyone familiar with the building knew you could walk into the lobby and up the stairs to any floor. My second-floor studio was twenty-five hundred square feet and New York shabby—big dirty windows, a fire escape with large steel locks. The Village location in the 10012 zip code was a plus. Pretty much every day before painting I'd ride my bike over to Washington Square Park. Then one night it was stolen. That thing of the city with its cracked sidewalk and the vivifying absence of order: something just mysteriously plucked. You knew people prowled around the Village at night with crowbars and cable cutters boosting whatever they could find.

There was a loud knock. Without even thinking, I turned the knob and voilà, there he was, standing in the doorframe. Only three months had passed since we'd been husband and wife. But he looked different— kind of flashy and shabby at once. Out of control, as if he'd focused on his hair and fingers but forgotten to wear a shirt.

"Listen." He pushed into the room. "I've come to get my books and records."

"Books and records?" I said. "I don't know which ones are exclusively yours. I thought they were *our* books and records."

"Well, they're mine," he said, now coming completely into the room. Men have to exaggerate a point to truly believe it. "You never bought a book in your life."

This was not great. I felt my body tense, my pelvic muscles squeeze together. These sensations had come a couple of times before: when he threw a book at me right before I went into labor. Then, after I had begun to sell paintings. At a restaurant when he threw a salt shaker at me. Maybe he thought throwing was less offensive than a blow because there was no actual physical contact between us.

I was slightly built and he was over six feet tall and weighed more than two hundred pounds. You didn't want someone like him angry. Especially with no one else around.

Nor did I want him in my actual studio where work from the night was drying on the floor.

"Please don't go into my studio," I said, blocking him. "Stuff is still wet." He must have remembered this. "You know how that is."

"I will go wherever I want. Pat, I am an adult man, and I can go wherever I want. See? Here I am walking around your studio."

"But this is *my* studio. I pay the rent. You'll have to leave."

"Move over," he said, pushing me, and I could see little bubbles of sweat accumulating on his forehead. I remember looking at him at that moment, and what stunned me was his face was absolutely dry, as it had looked at certain moments of focus or large feeling with him. It was without expression. A kind of dry ecstasy of expressionlessness. It was in these moments of remote inhumanness that he often would suddenly lunge to the other pole, and I wanted to say, *Look, I'll leave you alone here and you go through the books and take whatever you want . . .* , but I couldn't trust him alone with the paintings. The show was two weeks away. What had amazed me, in the year leading up to our separation, was that he thought this was him at his most rational, when to anyone outside it was just the last stage before the absolute reverse. "You stole all my money out of our joint bank account and now you're telling me where I can go?" He said "booksandrecords" together like it was one word. Then he bent down and grabbed a lead pipe forgotten on the studio's floor.

The pipe had been left over from an electrical wiring job. Maybe the elevator guy had dropped it? In a studio you find all kinds of things, because anything can be helpful in the construction of a painting. You also might find large wooden cooking spoons to stir paint with, stepladders to look down at your paintings from, egg beaters for high-velocity and high-volume stirring, and spray guns to spray paint out of. What my husband found was this gray pipe.

The alarm in me peaked and I couldn't hear what he was saying exactly. Just that he was talking in that dry-skinned, forceful way that he always thought had such impressive clarity but that always seemed to other people as if he were having a fit, was in the grip of something unnatural. It's often when people think they are at their most eloquent that they are at their deepest, creepiest level of fixity and craziness.

I had become acquainted with that side of my husband in Vermont. So the alarm would raise and block out my hearing. I could feel it like heat over my ears, as if they were blushing over what they had to listen to. And then it dropped down, below ear level, and I would hear him talking: ". . . if you don't observe the *difference* between what you believe is yours and what is clearly mine, except only insofar as to the degree of deciding it should all be yours. . . ." And I would see his nostril flare and it was always that ridiculous, alarming thing of some men, to think they could suddenly pose as angels of reason outside their big, expectant, violent bodies. But even worse I knew that not being listened to was one of the accelerants for his anger—and knowing that kept causing alarm to blot out everything he was saying. So we were locked in, even though he, masturbating over his own eloquence, couldn't see that this is where he was taking us. The kids had always been there, though, as a brake. ". . . and I find in good conscience I cannot allow, I *cannot*. . . ."

"I'm just going to go out and come back in about twenty minutes. Or an hour. Will you listen? I am going to leave."

"Then how will we get this taken care of to *everybody's* mutual satisfaction like two rational *adults* who once loved each other?"

"Fine. So I will go outside and be back in sixty minutes."

He clapped his hands loudly to get my attention. Like smashing something small between meaty palms. I jumped. And that other side of him that assessed vulnerabilities—the side that looked for advantage, weakness, and ways to assert superiority—saw me jump, and I don't think he knew that he smiled.

"Pat! Hello? Are you listening?" He snapped his fingers as you would at a sleeper, or at someone under hypnosis. I don't think he knew the wicked things his face was doing then. The little smiles as I backed away. How . . . *hungry* he seemed, at this show of fear. The part of him that liked the feeling of winning, that needed it, must have realized: *this* was why he had come.

"I was your husband four months ago. You would *willingly*, Pat, most *willingly* put your head down beside *mine* on a pillow and we would mix our *breaths together* for a whole night and listen to each other's noises through the *toilet door* in the morning and now—" He clapped his hands again. "Look at how you jump! Do you *not* see how *insulting* that is *to me*? What a *grotesque in*sult this *is* to *me*?" The italics were coming closer and closer together—with a certain kind of person, the worst sign. You know what happens in a moment like this: you feel the depression, the undertow of the depression, that you once made this choice. That this was another hand in life you played badly.

". . . so I'm going out now," I said again. I couldn't process what he was saying. I started to walk quickly for the door.

And then he picked up the pipe and slammed it hard on the painting table. Like a gavel. I turned—the sound was so loud I thought he had perhaps hit me and my body was slow at transmitting the news of the impairment. I saw the pipe bouncing up from the painting table, and the plastic water dishes and paint tubes flying up in the air, and his smile at whatever was on my face. Maybe he thought it was to mock my fear that he raised the pipe over his head, as if for a great, smooth swing. And when I ran then, for the door, he crossed the room in three big strides and was chasing me.

I sprinted out and down the stairs. And when I returned with a friend twenty minutes later he was gone. In the distance we heard the wail of ambulance sirens.

42 WOOSTER

IN THE LATE 1960S AND 1970S, if you were an ambitious American visual artist, you had to be in SoHo. It was a neighborhood in transition. Big trucks carried bolts of colored cloth up and down crowded streets. (I learned recently that the word "mercer"—as in Mercer Street, one of SoHo's three main thoroughfares—means "a merchant who deals in textiles.")

Unlike the rest of the city, when we lived there SoHo had no amenities. Not even an occasional tree on the sidewalk. There was only one supermarket in the area, half a mile away on LaGuardia Place. You had to drag a shopping cart over cobblestones, as if you were back in a very primitive New York. The other food store was on the corner of Prince Street and West Broadway, an ancient bodega that periodically came alive at night for cockfights. I actually walked in once to buy something and on the floor saw chickens cruelly pecking at each other while men stood around yelling excitedly in Spanish. It turns out that in 1979 six-year-old Etan Patz was murdered in this very bodega. Finally after two trials Pedro Hernandez, who'd worked in the basement at the time, was charged with murder. He'd killed the little boy and then thrown the body into a garbage can like trash.

Eighty years before, in the 1880s, SoHo had been home to clothing merchants and textile factories. At the same time, lower Broadway was a luxury street full of fancy stores, theaters, and elegant homes. (Edith Wharton describes this area in *The House of Mirth*. She was actually born farther uptown, on Twenty-Third Street, in a building that now houses a Starbucks.) The three-block area, Mercer, Greene, and Wooster Streets, was between West Broadway and Broadway. As if they were words from a song I'd rhythmically chant the names to myself while walking around the neighborhood ("Mercer, Greene, Wooster").

It had been a red-light district in the late nineteenth century, when prostitution was accepted in New York City. Walt Whitman even wrote about this "general laxity" in *The Daily Times*.

From a guidebook of the period:

Miss Clara Gordon—No. 119 Mercer Street—We cannot too highly recommend this house. The lady herself is a perfect Venus: beautiful, entertaining, and supremely seductive. Her aides de camp are really charming and irresistible and altogether honest and honorable. Miss G. is a great belle, and southern merchants and planters patronize her mansion principally. She is highly accomplished, skillful, and prudent, and sees her visitors are well entertained. Good wines of the most elaborate brands [are] constantly on hand, and in all, a finer resort cannot be found in the City.

Ninety years later, when I moved in, the neighborhood's cast-iron and limestone buildings were white, dark gray, and beige. Cast iron had been used since the 1860s to cover preexisting structures and give the exteriors the look of stone. That material was chosen because it was thought to be fireproof. Which turned out not to be the case. In fact the area soon became known as Hell's Hundred Acres because there were so many fires. With cast iron, though, you could have large windows and heavily molded surfaces that still allowed for intricate columns on the facades. You even see these now. And since cast iron was manufactured in New York City, buildings could be put up quickly. But by the 1960s, manufacturing in SoHo had pretty much dried up: a 1962 report called the area the "Wasteland of New York." And that's when the first painters and sculptors started moving in. With low rents and poor living conditions—no heat or hot water—they could get by, albeit just barely.

Outside of low rent, the most important thing to a flourishing community of artists is space. SoHo had both. The Village, an artist's haven in the 1940s and '50s, had become crowded and expensive. But south of Houston Street, as manufacturing had dwindled, there were acres and acres of "raw space." My generation of artists pioneered these lofts and created "SoHo." We forged and welded and wall-removed live-work lofts out of abandoned factories. We had taken that old factory history and turned it into play—a different architectural sort of masquerading.

In addition to everything else, for people then in their late twenties and early thirties living in SoHo had the advantage of being an automatic put-down of your parents' values, a real "fuck you" to their sense of scale—their discrete rooms in houses with treed backyards. We were done with that. Instead, we embraced free-flowing spaces, which went along with free-flowing sex. There was no one room for sex either: you could engage anywhere in the open area of the loft and then—wherever, but still inside—meander over to your big studio and do a grand American-type abstraction. At the same time, collectors had been browbeaten into thinking that if they didn't rearrange their furniture to accommodate your huge painting, they weren't worthy of the name. The painting was no longer a sedate object on the wall. It had become the wall.

The buildings in SoHo usually had five stories connected in the interior by wide wooden staircases. And there were huge freight elevators too, which opened onto each floor. (Once, an inebriated artist, Ilya Bolotowsky, opened his elevator door when the cab wasn't there and plunged to his death.)

I rented a loft on Wooster Street between Grand and Broome. It was made of brick rather than the usual cast iron. There was even a brick staircase leading up to the front door, where the number 42 was boldly printed in black. After I moved in, the huge space had to be transformed into a classic artist's loft, circa 1972: five thousand square feet into a home. That took about six months. The landlord, a short Jewish guy named Steve Weinberg, had given me a couple months rent-free so I could do the renovation. He'd rented the space to me as commercial, because it didn't comply with the city's residential codes, but he knew I'd be living there with my two sons. We had left the house in the country and I'd found the loft that was then built from scratch so we could all live there. The boys went to the Village Community School on Christopher Street in the Village. ("Commercial" and "residential" were the two words that decided your fate then: Would your lease allow you to live and work in the same space?) My lease meant that if the city showed up I could be kicked out at any moment. But the authorities didn't come around much.

Ken, whom I was dating at the time, knew how to put a loft together; he'd worked on several SoHo crews who were then transforming the neighborhood. What it took was Sheetrock, polyurethane, plumbing, and lots of cursing. The basic words and phrases of that moment were "This is bullshit," "fucking asshole," "motherfucker," and "schmuck." Swearing was so prevalent that David got the idea all grown-ups spoke that way and thought something was wrong when he heard an adult conversation where no one cursed.

The whole dusty five-thousand-square-foot room, with its high ceilings and huge, twelve-foot windows, needed walls that would define a kitchen, bathroom, studio, and places to sleep. It needed lights and a water supply. It needed fixtures. And furniture.

Off to one side we created a big square painting space, which was defined by the large columns that ran down the loft's center. Every floor had them; interior columns had been part of New York City factory construction in the late nineteenth century.

A SMALL AREA near the entrance was set aside for my bedroom; the kitchen was up front, where the windows faced the street, and the children's bedroom, which had thick glass walls, was in the middle section of the loft. The bathroom was off in one corner up front, where the necessary plumbing already existed. The last step was laying down a wooden floor and then applying two coats of polyurethane. Because the floors needed a couple days to dry, we had to stay at Ken's loft on Crosby Street. Returning, we stepped into a big white space replete with track lighting, a new Parsons table, and a full kitchen (traded for a painting).

No one else lived in our building. The cloth factories continued to run on other floors. And at night, when the workers left, it felt a little like the Frank family hideout in Amsterdam. I was frightened returning home late—walking down the dark, desolate street alone and then up the outside flight of brick stairs. When I took a cab the driver would often wait outside, until he saw me wave from the kitchen window.

Once my father visited. I was in therapy at the time. When I told my shrink, a few days later, that my father had paid for the kitchen cabinets, delivered while he was there, he criticized me. "By accepting money from your father you allow yourself to become dependent on him." Later, though, when I had no money to pay for therapy, the therapist dropped me like a hot potato.

I remember my father looking out the front windows onto Wooster Street. He pointed, nodding, to the other side of the street: "I used to work in a birdcage factory right there, number 37, when I was ten," he said.

In fact, moving downtown had put me in touch with the Lower East Side where he grew up—swimming in the East River, eating graham crackers at Gouverneur Hospital—he'd been treated there for pneumonia—playing hooky. I've since learned from George Bellows's paintings that the East River was a big neighborhood swimming hangout. My father had described the Lower East Side as if he were Huck Finn and the East River the Mississippi.

THERE WAS NO special attitude toward weekends in SoHo, no "Have a nice weekend." Every day was the same. You worked, drank, and stayed up late. The most important thing was total disdain for anything that

smacked of bourgeois behavior. My generation considered itself hip—
not like our parents and their friends. And yet now people talk about
my generation as if we were from the 1930s. "The husbands from that
era are hard on their wives," I read in the newspaper recently. What?
Guys who used to wear bell-bottoms, with shaggy hair and beards, are
hard on their wives? In the end, every generation turns out to be the
same; they just wore different clothes.

DIRT, STONE, BRICK, SMASHED MIRRORS

THERE WERE TWO CHOICES for dinner at Max's Kansas City: lobster or steak. I always ordered steak. My boyfriend favored lobster. He never paid the tab. After a year or so he gave the owner a sculpture.

Max's was just north of the Village. Taxi was the preferred mode of arrival. If you lived nearby, it was fine to walk through the surrounding area, which was a wasteland, but the second your driver made that right off Seventeenth Street, there was the oasis of light framed in the club's big window, and at that moment it felt like catching a reflection of your truest, most energized self in the mirror.

You learned the contradictions: the club's owner wasn't named Max—he was a hard-partying man called Mickey. Tall with long, straight black hair and a downturned nose like the nose of a dwarf in a story. Plus a slightly discolored, chipped tooth. He was also unaffiliated with Kansas City. Nearly every night you got out of the cab and walked in there'd be Larry Poons; cheery, noisy, and already drunk Dan Christiansen; and sly, calculating, and handsome Peter Reginato. You got to know what to expect. The famous car-wreck sculptor John Chamberlain hunched at the bar in his jeans and dark polo; Frosty Meyers, with his punk haircut and walrus mustache; and Larry Zox, heavyset, his wavy hair swept back, signaling for the bartender. Macho guys. When you're young, you expect to mostly mix with others who are young. And then are surprised by the range of ages—late twenties to early forties. The range of backgrounds that brought everyone in was the life of art. And Mickey Ruskin, the non-Kansas non-Max, who had been a lawyer and had then determined, somehow, that life should present one more exciting offer, and had had this wish granted. Art had welcomed him in too.

Mickey, often smiling, had renounced all the sharkiness of his former profession. Even on the issue of billing. Whatever the artists ate and drank was on account. Nobody ever paid. As soon as the number reached into the low thousands they gave Mickey art. Installations dotted the club; it was like a museum, paintings and sculpture that secretly commemorated the appetites.

You'd see women as you entered the bar, felt yourself being swallowed up by heat and body smell and the sour mash of the alcohol and the pepper from everybody's cigarettes, in a wham plus the thump and noise of the music. It was like entering some other absolutely consuming element: jumping into a still and warm ocean. That first moment, then accommodating yourself. Some small number of women were painters like me. Many were plus-ones—women on various arms, posing and temporary, there for generalized love of art or love for some particular and passing artist. Painters were mostly men. The sculptors were always men. You could tell them by the stains on their jeans—acetylene for the sculptors, acrylic and glue for the painters—and by the color under the painters' fingernails. Max's wasn't just a restaurant. It was a museum of unpaid tabs. And it was also a fellowship.

You'd push past Frosty Myers and John Chamberlin, up to Mickey's face behind the bar, in a dark blue sweater, wiping out a wineglass with his long, soiled dish towel. The times I spoke with him at length did not go well. He always seemed to have his attention drifting elsewhere—somewhere above my words or to one side of the conversation, receiving signals from a calm elsewhere, until finally you stopped trying. Or someone found you and explained about Mickey and drugs, and how he was always just the same, he was like that with everybody.

Above the thumping music everyone shouted to be heard. To be appreciated, recognized, seen for a night, all of it coiling around as you sipped wine, grinned, unstuck lips from your teeth, lit a cigarette, knowing inside the inhale you were smiling. There was the overall calming feeling then: usually in life there is a right place to be. Sometimes you find out too late. Or you never knew about it. Or this right place was inaccessible—you were not cool enough, rich enough, enough, enough. So to find yourself, on a night in Max's in that unimpeachably right place, with the right people, at the right time: this was unspeakably soothing. It was to be without want. Without ambivalence. To know that the club owner knew you. Knew your boyfriend, your friends, your individual preferences, operated the famous club for all of us. It was an amazingly tactful and fortifying compliment, paid to us every night.

Talk was monosyllables. Bellowed through cupped hands. You're here! Yes! Came with Poons? Good. Come over here! How are you? Good! Thanks! You look great! No, I already have one! Everybody's back here! What? We're all here, we're all back here!

JOHN CHAMBERLAIN HAD deep creases in his face. They crinkled whenever he laughed. He laughed a lot. I thought it was because of all the money he was making from those crushed automobile panels he turned into sculpture. Sometimes I'd sit in his red booth, across from that round, lined face, and laugh right along with him. You didn't need to have a reason. We could smile that way for a night, looking around at the club, sawing at our steaks, filling an ashtray—and then realize later that we'd never said a word.

And then you wandered past the big central area of red booths, into the smells of dinner and the irrelevant meals floating on platters above the waitress's shoulders, past the nonartist eaters who also came to the club. And then at the far end of the restaurant was Andy.

Warhol and his entourage holed up in Mickey's private room, around a huge circular table. But it was their club too. That they had been drawn here by the same noisy power source we were drawn to was strange. The Factory people dressed in wild getups with exotic, creatively teased hairdos. You didn't know if they were armed. Dan Christensen believed some of them were packing guns. And when you looked you saw this could conceivably be right. Everyone close to Warhol had become skittish after the experience with Valerie Solanas. She had ridden the Factory elevator, fishing in her handbag where she had two guns, caught sight of Andy, and squeezed off three rounds, one finding and piercing her target through his slender torso. Sometimes at Max's, Andy would unbutton his shirt and show the scar as if it were an old war wound. That had been only a few years before. They seemed not to know what else to expect, and there was hostility from our side: we didn't consider the Factory people artists. Pop art was an affront and insult to the more difficult and serious thing we understood ourselves to be doing.

Some people are attracted to art for the chance to live like outlaws: outside the Monday and Friday margins, the hashmarks of nine and five. They do the minimum necessary work to qualify and really hope their lives will be the art. I hadn't come for the oddness of the art world. It was different for me at night: then I was as restless as anybody else. But my daytime model was Matisse, who painted in a business suit.

For us, Andy wasn't an artist. He was something—a force, a figurehead, a *showman*. He didn't paint—his work was in silkscreen. He hated, he said, the act of painting. Soon we feasted on details of his former existence. How Andy had started by drawing shoes for Bonwit Teller until he realized there was quite a bit more to be made doing the exact same thing in the art world. Then he started doing the shoes, not as ads but as silkscreens. We wondered about his cow fixation, which was apparent in an exhibition of his cow wallpaper at the Whitney. (Along with floating silver balloons.) Then we learned that his uncle had been a milkman. So there was respect and hostility. Hostility: if you are an artist, anybody else getting attention as an artist is a hazard.

The amount of money and attention is limited. That anger, that sense of flat injustice in the appreciation of others, is one of the world's first signs that you are an artist. And there was the respect, the business acknowledgment: the pop artists had found this surprising and direct route to money.

These thoughts could sometimes make Max's feel sadder. A moment when the wheels came off and the chassis sat there and you realized the art world was a small place bounded by compromise and disappointment. It chilled you, a thought of this nature, like a wind. And you'd duck your nose into your wineglass or refill your lungs with cigarette smoke until even the backwash of that feeling went away. And after a few minutes some sensation or person distracted you, and the gray unwelcome sense was gone.

BOB DYLAN PLAYED Madison Square Garden, and somebody got me tickets. By chance I landed a great seat, very close and a little to one side. There was Andy, standing, leaning. His tall, almost model-thin body against the wall right near my seat. The eyes behind his glasses rested half-closed as he stared straight ahead with his deadpan, unchanging look. He was there so many of my other nights that I was not surprised to find him on an evening when I wasn't at Max's. His blond wig had the consistency of straw: the affect so diminished that after a while he seemed a kind of urban scarecrow.

He stood alone the whole concert. His expression never changed. Perhaps he was waiting for someone to snap a picture. You couldn't not be aware of him. That weird neutral presence. I never found out why he was standing by my seat, who or what he had expected.

I TRIED TO EXPLAIN THIS to my Florida dealer, Dorothy Blau. She and Andy were tight. It was that thing, then, of Andy being around. I could tell Dorothy wasn't exactly listening. Once I'd said his name, she was just waiting me out. She had something she wanted to say. "Oh, doll, it's funny you should bring him up. I just heard from Andy," she said.

"Why?" I asked. I wondered if Andy knew we shared a Florida dealer. Or if he had already mentioned to her coming out that night for Dylan and finding himself standing near me.

"So last week I go to The Factory. You know, Andy has his cosmetician waiting to take care of my makeup. Well, she does a very excellent job, such a nice job. Then he snaps two pictures of me for a silk screen."

She waited. When I didn't say anything fast enough, her style of waiting became a little affronted.

"Did his cosmetician do your makeup wrong?" I finally asked.

"No, doll, you aren't getting it. I had arranged for just one portrait. I thought it would be the one, a silk screen like the Jackie O. But he gets on the phone just now, all wispy and Andy and innocent: 'Hi Dotty. Both your portraits are ready.' Both! So he's proposing to charge me twenty thousand for the two of them, or fourteen if I go ahead and let him down and take only one."

I wanted to say, *What a hustler.* To ask, *Why would Andy, with all those Factory people, need to chisel an extra six thousand dollars out of our sweet and bubbly Miami dealer?*

I told her to stick to her guns. If Dorothy remembered only asking for one portrait, then buy only that one. "Doll," I said, "be true to yourself." I was always surprised, talking with Dorothy, that I could get away with words like "doll." Did she really think that was a word I otherwise ever used? But people usually liked the compliment of you talking like them.

Dorothy bought both, worth millions now probably. Far more than paintings by any of us in the front room who had thought of Andy as the backroom embarrassment, as our nightly inconvenience.

You'd see handsome Bob Mapplethorpe, who came with a black-haired and thin woman, Patti Smith. Their plans already incorporated the power shift we couldn't quite feel taking place under our feet. That Andy, with his energy-free persona in the back of the restaurant, was going to dominate. Patti Smith would write later about the military campaigns she plotted with Robert: how to penetrate the defenses around Andy's table at Max's. How to traverse the big main room. When would be the best time to approach Andy? Which day and hour? How should Bob dress? What should Patti be wearing when that right time came?

Our tables—where the noisy group of us painters and sculptors spilled drinks and smelled that stinging cut of alcohol on the backs of our hands and tried to make ourselves heard over the din—were just the area she and Robert had to cross on their journey to Andy's table.

There was music playing. Part of the job of songs is to keep you from noticing your gathering fate. That you are aging, that you are less central than you imagine. Max's house band—they played in his basement—was the Velvet Underground. So rising from your feet, always, the slowed-down vocals and dragging chords: "Linger *on*, your *pale* blue eyes. . . ." "Sweet *Jane*. . . ." Lou Reed and Nico; their music had something. You'd walk downstairs and see shadows swaying. But when you paused upstairs and listened, that music was correct for the moment. Sad, romantic, and overripe.

ROBERT SMITHSON AND CARL ANDRE were also at the bar. Their dress code was scruffy modern—heavy denim overalls over work shirts. Clothes advertise the tone of your work: their pieces seemed to derive from a disappointed construction site. Smashed mirrors, dirt, stone, brick. Every night their lumpy bodies occupying our bar. Those encroachers. They were called only by their last names. Smithson and Andre, like partners in a detective agency.

Smithson was tall and black-haired, with skin pitted like a poorly paved road. Andre was shorter and heavyset, with a long beard and pugnacious face. Until Smithson's death—a summer plane crash in Texas; I pictured a cactus, then the crash—the men were inseparable. After that, death seemed to be stalking Andre. A decade later his wife plummeted out of their thirty-fourth-floor window. Andre stood trial for three years, then was found innocent. He got off. By that time Max's was over. We were over too. There was no proper place to be with everyone to talk *about* Andre's surprising release, though it would have been interesting to see the face of a man who had perhaps committed murder and had just had his freedom, surprisingly, restored to him.

Mickey had closed the bar. He tried another, too far downtown. Nobody went. He died of an overdose, in bed. As gone then as Robert Smithson and Carl Andre's wife.

ALL THE DIFFERENT art groups attracted to Max's hated each other. The tension between the conceptual artists, the land-matter artists, and my own hands-on, abstraction painter-sculptor group could become fraught. Artists competing for something incredibly valuable and very limited. Money, attention, validation. It felt like the next thing was a fight, which could erupt at any moment.

One night, I finally tried the lobster. I didn't know what it had to do with Max or Kansas City, but it had always been there on the menu, so I ordered it.

I was sitting across from Ken Greenleaf, my boyfriend. He'd been on the cover of the *New York Times Magazine*, representing the new sculpture. Ken's face was shiny with grease. He was sawing at his meat with the thick-handled knives Mickey preferred. And sometimes he delicately patted his lips with the bandanna he wore around his neck.

Then he put down the knife and got quiet. The air between all the groups had become supercharged, as it does before a storm. Sounds turned strangely distinct. Silver and glasses. People's walks became heavy-footed and exaggerated. Smithson thumped past our table in his thick boots. Ken was now quietly and roughly drying his fingers with the napkin.

It was so quick. The booted thump, and then Smithson had pulled Dan Christensen away from the bar by his shoulder and was pistoning his closed fist into Dan's face. Dan slipped and kicked over his stool. Then Frosty Meyers was reaching around Smithson and I said, "Call someone." But Ken was already among the twisting men. Carl

Andre wrapped his short, meaty arms around Frosty Meyers. The men stayed together, and three skinny figures darted out from Andy's room at the back of the club. Soon ten men were spinning together on the floor, elbows thumping on the floorboards, upending barstools, sending chairs to make their rumbling, protesting noise as they skittered across the club's floor. I remember John Chamberlin, still grinning, stepping far away from the pile. I remember Dan's big thigh muscle showing through his jeans as he kicked Smithson twice in the side.

It couldn't have lasted more than a few minutes. Then Mickey's staff was pulling red-faced men apart. Dan was swollen and breathing heavily. And the tall and strange-looking men from The Factory were pulled away, looking sourly back at us. They'd never said a word. Just retreated to their own precincts. Mickey made some kind of speech—you couldn't translate the sentences, but it was just the right calming sounds, when suddenly everything had been so present and combustible.

Ken and I stood outside with Dan Christensen. October city wind cooled our skin. Dan was swollen-faced, breathing hard. He kept smiling and letting his mouth go slack, remembering different moments as he regained control of his breathing. He was a little drunk. He grinned again. "Huh," Dan said. "So they turned out not to be packing after all."

"No," Ken said.

"Don't know why Mickey had to break it up," Dan said. "We could've taken them."

It was dark and quiet outside on Seventeenth Street. A cab and a bus streaked by. I said he was right. Dan's breathing was now mostly in its regular rhythm.

"Yeah, we took them," he decided.

"Yeah, let's go back in," Ken agreed.

SANDWICHES

AFTER, WHEN WE HAD left the neighborhood forever and life had become quiet and difficult, I thought about the parties. Every day in SoHo was the same: you worked, drank, stayed up late. Weekends didn't matter. So parties came on Tuesday or Thursday, after openings.

The whole pregame ritual of it—pulling on jeans and a sweater, doing your makeup over the bathroom sink, with particular attention to mascara. Some makeup consultants had told me to always brush green or brown eyeshadow onto my large eyelids, and I did that. Then I'd draw a dark pencil line under my cheekbones, rubbing it into my face to make my cheekbones appear higher.

Usually the party was somewhere in our neighborhood. Or in the neighborhood that had no name—now called TriBeCa. The streets were Duane, Franklin, Reade, Mercer, Broome, and Desbrosses. Factory-sounding names that suggested iron-colored streets. And the hallways and stairs of these loft buildings were all the same. Painted gray—middle gray if you were buying the color—or sometimes a creepy, defeated industrial green. That green of institutions that had folded long ago. Without much light on the stairs. One dusty bulb in a dangling socket.

Entrances to these loft buildings were like the entrances of Paris apartment buildings—you were buzzed in. Usually, in SoHo then, this buzzer was broken and hung from its brass fitting like a loose tooth from an injured face. In Paris you'd punch in a code—which the

Parisians were able to remember or had written down in their excellent little leather notebooks. In SoHo, you'd simply yell to your upstairs
friend, who'd throw down, with a metal splash, their starfish of keys.

Once inside, you'd start climbing those wide, cold, lonely stairs, dig-
ging your hands into gloves or coat pockets. Winding the scarf tighter
around your neck and cold hair. In winter these staircases seemed
endless, your heels pounding the steps, visible breath warming your
face. Even socks felt cold on these SoHo staircases. Then you knocked
when you guessed you had reached the right door.

If you'd counted the floors correctly, there would be the big clunky
noise of the police lock unbolting. Every loft space had one—the only
serious protection available against burglary. At that time police weren't
interested in SoHo. The tall double doors made of heavy metal swung
out onto the hall. This made every loft feel like a fortified bohemian
castle with a heavy, impenetrable gate. Inside it would be dark. With
some candles burning on the hors d'oeuvres table—revealing plates of
shiny olives—or set in saucers and flickering around the room. Definitely loud music—very often the Rolling Stones, always Dylan, occasionally Janis Joplin. These were men who worked with their hands
and knew how to set stereos for maximum effect. Speakers hung from
the ceiling in complicated arrangements, sometimes perched like a
surrealist statement on the top step of ladders. The wood floors, even
in the dark, were glossy from layers of polyurethane. Which everyone
applied to their floorboards as the old masters had brushed varnish
onto their court portraits.

There was an art to living. Where to put bed and bathroom, where to
install shower and refrigerator in these spaces we'd all inherited from
the factories. And many times, on studio visits to friends, when I didn't
entirely love the work I would exclaim, "Beautiful loft," as if the true
artwork had been the ingenious ways they had found to fix their lofts.

Ceilings were always high. Which we filled with smoke and music. A
studio table waited to the right of the door, tablecloth pinned down at
each corner by liquor bottles. Like the painting by Manet of the Folies
Bergère bar, but minus the woman.

AT THESE PARTIES, you might or might not talk. Same vibe as Max's. Talking wasn't that big. Dancing was big. Sex. All the time, from the corner of an eye, you were monitoring the party, trying to reach a decision about who in the loft your next lover might be.

There would be kids there too. Never many. Very few of us had risked the competing investment of children. Mine were usually home at our loft, presumably under blankets in their vast bedroom, whose ceiling was a maze of right-angled sprinkler pipes. Part of my own real estate genius had been to convert our space's back half into another living space, which I then rented to a young couple. This arrangement was supposed to include in situ babysitting. They were, in their bland and academic way, a nice graduate student couple. I learned much later that the blandness had terrified my children, who had never known people in SoHo to be so normal and mild in manner, and suspected them of innumerable dangerous hungers and secrets.

The same crew from the club. It was as if we couldn't get enough of each other. Frosty Meyers and Larry Poons, Larry Zox, and Peter Reginato, who proved every time you saw him that you could be handsome in a shifty way; the unctuous sculptor Michael Steiner with his clingy girlfriend, Elissa. You knew the party was nearly over—that guests were patting and investigating the bed on which everybody had dumped their coats in a mound—when she would wander around the loft asking, "Has anyone seen Michael?"

Dan Christensen, with his solid, friendly looks. Some nights also his girlfriend, Cynthia Something. The last thing these men seemed to be after was the company of their current women. In general, whoever you arrived with was quickly dropped. An attentive date was a liability. At the end you'd check to see if your date had stayed. Often they hadn't. Or you might see them across the loft, an arm around someone else. If so, you'd head home alone, and reconnect sometime the next day.

Strange things happened at parties.

One night—this was in my own giant space with my own children free roamers in the smoke and music—Larry Poons became convinced police had tailed him upstairs. He believed they had melded in with the guests, and were even then making their stealthy way forward to arrest him. Someone had put the needle on Dylan's "Like a Rolling Stone." This was a song, whatever the mood, that always made me wary. How fast things could go rotten. It was a taunt. "To be on your own," Dylan warned. "No direction home—a complete unknown." I wonder if I was the only one secretly afraid this could happen to me. Larry had dropped to my floor, with his thick, wild hair and his legs stretched out in front of him.

"They're here," Larry kept insisting. "And will arrest me without joy, warrant, or pity. They will be swift and they will prove merciless." But Larry was subject to whims and pressures none of us could fathom. So we all began checking rooms for him. Bathroom, studio, even the boys' room. All proved definitely police-free. Somebody got out my big flashlight, one of those powerful beams with a virtual briefcase of batteries, and swung it around the space, across surprised faces and spread, dancing fingers. To show that all was safe, no badges were in attendance.

"Yes but," Larry said, "they could be plainclothesmen."

André Emmerich, my dealer, was also Helen Frankenthaler's, one of the most powerful art figures in the city. It made us all proud and relieved to spot him at a party. Later, I went into my bedroom and there André was: reading glasses on, sitting at my desk with a prim library expression and flipping through a book of Hieronymus Bosch reproductions.

"Aren't you going"—I thought of how to put this—"to enjoy the party?"

His eyebrows lifted. "Oh . . . ," he said. "I am very comfortable right here, Pat." But then he smiled, closed the book, raised himself from my desk on his thick knuckles, and walked into the noise. When I looked around a quarter hour later he was nowhere to be found.

THERE WERE ALWAYS people from the neighborhood. People you didn't know or didn't want to. This was okay. They were friends with somebody. Or had heard the music and wandered in and could tell you of a distant, and perhaps even better, party. Only in the early morning, when it was time to leave, did the lights come on. Then, blinking, you could see the whole tired room, its ceiling pipes and radiators and floors—like an aging beauty, these spaces relied on the modesty of darkness. At this 2:00 a.m. hour, some people would have already left for the bars—Ken and John's on Broome Street, or the Spring Street Bar over on the corner of West Broadway. We all had tabs there too. Not much paper money got exchanged in SoHo.

The stairs were always easier on the way down. You bounced down, all sweaty and warm from alcohol and dancing. We'd take off together for the bars. All of us now out on the winter street, which also seemed warmer when you were drunk and in a crowd. We were artists. This was our city, our streets, our neighborhood, our profession. There'd be cigarettes lighting up with their sparks and hisses followed by long exhales. The squeak, if it had snowed, of snow under everybody's boots. You'd flash on other parts of your life in a moment like this and know it had all been okay, if it gave you access to these lovely moments, surrounded by friends and colleagues, in a part of the city owned equally by all of you.

At the bar friends ordered burgers. I had read something about cat food being used in burgers and ordered something else. More joking; more talking about nothing. Then I'd go home. Stairs, musical keys, police lock. In a few hours, it would be seven, and I could wake Jon and David, get their sandwiches ready for school. Baloney and cheese, peanut butter and jelly. I'd be bleary-eyed, sitting at the Parsons table trying to make conversation, checking to see if they had their bus passes. Then I'd kiss them goodbye. As they walked down the brick stairs they'd say stuff like, "You know what Mom said?" "No, really, Mom said that?" And then they'd bump into each other as they made their way down the outside stairs.

FALLING OFF

IT WAS AROUND two in the afternoon, and I was walking down East Eighty-Second Street toward the Met.

Coming in the opposite direction I saw a man around my height who looked to be in his early seventies. I thought maybe it was the art critic Clement Greenberg, whom I'd met a couple times before, first at Emmerich Gallery in the late sixties and then more recently at Bennington College, where he'd given a series of lectures. As we got closer I saw it *was* him.

"Mr. Greenberg," I said. "Hi, how are you?"

"The same," he answered. (I learned later he always gave that answer, implying nothing had really improved in the art world.)

Greenberg was wearing a soiled orange parka that came down below his hips, and one of those English checked wool and tweed walking caps. "How are *you*, Pat? And please call me Clem," he said.

"I will," I said. "I'm okay. Living uptown now, painting."

IN TRUTH, the early '80s were a low point for both of us. Since I'd attended his Bennington lectures a few years earlier, the only positive thing to happen was my son David's return to New York in 1979. He was back living with me and starting high school. On the other hand my painting career needed mouth-to-mouth resuscitation. People I'd known just a few years before crossed to the other side of the street when they saw me. But perhaps that was going to change now, because standing right in front of me was this famous art critic, and he was holding ground.

It wasn't the greatest time for him either. After his art criticism had dominated the New York art world for over three decades, a new group of figurative artists had come in: Julian Schnabel with his plates, David Salle with his porn in black and white. Plus some Italian artists who painted wild animals and schmeared distorted figures onto canvas. Which had pushed modernism and the formalists, with whom Greenberg identified, aside. His daughter, a student at Vassar, had reported back to Clem her art history professor's evaluation: "Greenberg," he said, "has been finished for ten years." (Making *his* cutoff date 1972.) Clem's advice to her was, "Don't say anything. You never defend a relative."

Over his four-decade career, Greenberg had acquired many enemies—artists he'd told the truth to about their work, and critics whose writing he'd disparaged. Now, with this changing of the guard, they were crawling out of the woodwork to publicly denounce him.

"WHAT DID YOU see at the museum, Clem?" I asked.

"France in the Golden Age," he replied, "curated by that guy from the Louvre, Pierre Rosenberg. It had some good things, but, damn, the pictures were hung too close together. Listen, Pat, I'd like to see what you're doing. Why don't you send me some slides?"

"Okay, great. I will," I said.

Clem tore a piece of paper from his notepad and wrote down his address in Norwich, New York. He'd left the city a few years before to live in the country full-time. Perhaps this move was to avoid the current art world situation?

Back home I looked at slides of my recent pictures. My photographer had shot them a few weeks before. At the time they'd looked fine, but now in light of this new development, they weren't holding up. The accompanying note would be delicate to write. Any wrong phrase or presumptuous remark could jeopardize this fragile beginning. I asked a writer friend to help, and we came up with something passable. The next day I mailed off a large tan envelope to Norwich.

Then the waiting, something I wasn't good at. Finally about a month later a light green envelope appeared. On the same color stationery, his typed letter was short and to the point. "In the main, from what I can see in the slides you are doing high art."

High art: even then it was a dated term, the pendulum having swung from pure modernism to turgid figuration. Still I was jubilant. It was so T. S. Eliot.

I FIRST HEARD Greenberg speak at Bennington College in 1971 when I'd been living in the godforsaken town of Hoosick Falls near the Vermont–New York border with my then husband and our two small children. It was the year after my initial art-world success. Seventy-one paintings of mine had sold at Emmerich Gallery. It was my husband who decided we had to leave New York. He wanted to become a writer. (Writer or painter, all you needed was the time so you could just quit your day job and try.) Instead, the town became the morgue of our marriage, the end of our small family.

But there was one positive, tiny thing: on a poster somewhere I'd read that the art critic Clement Greenberg would be giving five lectures at Bennington College. (Of course I knew who he was, everyone in the art world did, the most important American art critic of our time.) The first night I was stunned to hear Greenberg say, "Everything Robert Rauschenberg does is safe, easy, and conventional. His work is so mediocre. It's all about iconography, the Kennedys, Michelangelo, whose finger is touching whose." For the previous nine years I'd only heard raves about Rauschenberg, as if he were the new Picasso. It started in college with my art history professor, who also doubled as curator at the Jewish Museum. Professor Solomon sent me to see Rauschenberg's *Monogram* (*the goat with tire*). I hated it and also the picture *Canyon*, which had a dead bird glued to its surface. (What if the eagle fell off while you were looking?) After the initial shock—"Oh, look a dead bird on a painting, a goat with a tire in a museum!"—there was nothing to look at.

Clem spoke to perceptions I'd had for years. We saw eye to eye on many things. Like how trivial and boring both pop art and minimalism were.

There was also his charisma and electrifying smile.

He told me that as a young man he'd tried writing poetry. And that he could draw photographically. But in college his art came into conflict with literature and philosophy. When, in the late forties, he finally gave himself over to art criticism, it was as if Ernest Hemingway were writing the reviews. Clem was dazzling in conversation, weighed every word, and if necessary, circled back to correct something he'd said earlier ("I was wrong there, I should have said—"). I'd never met anyone as smart.

IN THE MID-EIGHTIES, Susan Sontag had a panel about the first art critic, Dennis Diderot. Catherine, the czarina of Russia, had summoned him to act as her art advisor. Which added to her collection at the Hermitage Museum.

That afternoon there were five panelists: Leon Golub, Donald Kuspit, Carter Ratcliff, Donald Judd, and Clem. I remember Judd having a small ponytail; he read some of his art reviews to the group. After which, getting back to Diderot, he said, "There is no more famous art critic here today than Mr. Greenberg."

Immediately Greenberg shot back, "Critics don't mean a damn. It's the worst art critics who think that criticism is very important."

Leon Golub then said, "All art criticism does is commodify art."

Clem seemed to be playing to the audience, leaning on shock value, the very thing he hated most in art. (He referred to the inventor of artistic shock value, Marcel Duchamp, as "the enemy of art.") When it was Clem's turn to speak, instead of reading his prepared statement, he simply said, "I'm bored stiff." And then, "I should have known better than to come."

Attempting to salvage the situation, Sontag began a discussion on why Diderot was important. She concluded with: "He was such a great critic—it's not even important which pictures he wrote about."

From the audience I raised my hand. "If Diderot were such a good critic," I said, "wouldn't he have picked the best paintings of his time?"

From the panel, Clem flashed his contagious smile. "That's a great question," he said.

WHEN I WAS TEACHING at a college in Connecticut, a tenure-track gig I'd nailed in 1983, I invited Clem to lecture there. Six years before, he'd given a talk at the nearby Wadsworth Atheneum from which the town was still recovering. I'd been in the audience that evening. "Trendiness came in," he said, "when the standards in art became avant-gardist. . . . After Pollock. . . . The best new art was supposed to shock. . . . What was required were spectacular effects. . . . Now the ticket to admission, to a place in art, has to be won by shock." And then his evaluation of the Tremaine Collection, which he'd been invited to speak about. Looking around the darkened auditorium, Clem said, "The Tremaine Collection is a document to trendiness." There were gasps from the audience, and the Tremaines simply got up and walked out of the auditorium.

His lecture and the meetings with my art students were free of shock value. He seemed energized by the questions they asked. Afterward we went for drinks. I'd invited Clem's old friend, the director of a New Haven museum, to join us. We arrived at the restaurant at the appointed 9:00 p.m., but the director was nowhere in sight. Finally, at 10:30, McDonnell and his blond, frizzy-haired date showed up. As he and Clem spoke about art and gossip, the dynamic heated up. Then Clem asked a question about a contemporary sculptor they both knew and McDonnell stopped the conversation, making it clear he didn't want to continue talking. Clem leaned across the table and said, "The trouble with you, Steven, is you don't have enough opinions."

THE NEXT DAY Clem and I drove back from Hartford, me at the wheel. I'd done the drive a million times, but having him in the passenger seat changed everything. What if, like Michel Gallimard—scion of the famous French publishing house—whose passenger one bleak January day had been Albert Camus, I crashed the car? The art world was rife with car deaths, from Jackson Pollock to David Smith.

It felt intimate being next to him in the front seat. I could sense him fishing around for conversation topics just like I was. Then I saw it from the outside, me driving this dazzling man, the smartest person I'd ever known, back to New York, the center of the world. He'd lived it, from Brooklyn to the Village to Central Park West. As had I.

BACK IN MANHATTAN, when I visited his apartment there was a new maid. It was the middle of April and he'd been complaining of shortness of breath. He took down a book by Kierkegaard and I took out my Nietzsche, *Beyond Good and Evil*. Sometimes we'd just sit for hours reading. Often in his study, where he could smoke. Or in my apartment after he'd looked at my pictures.

Clem was sitting in profile and looked like a George Grosz. I took out my notebook and did a fast sketch. Occasionally I'd look up and there'd be a light around his head, an aura emanating from it. That's when I had this scary thought that he wouldn't be there, sitting in that chair, in a short time. (Actually it took a year.) *I'll look in this room and he won't be there anymore,* I wrote down in the notebook. But after he died, I never went back to his study, so I didn't get to see the chair without him.

CLEM HAD A DATE for every painter, sculptor, poet—he thought the word "artist" was pretentious. The moment when they had fallen off.

For Rothko, 1955. And Reinhardt, that same bad year. The way I learned this was pure Clem. I was at MoMA—the big central escalator gave it the feel of a mall visit—for the Reinhardt retrospective. The pictures he did in the first half of the fifties looked very strong to me. I called Clem from a museum pay phone: "How come Reinhardt is so good between 1950 and 1955?" Clem answered, "Oh that's when he was friendly with Rothko. After that Rothko dropped him."

With Paul Klee, the bad calendar year was 1930—"when he started using thick black outlines," Clem said. Picasso was clear until 1918, after which "he never did a good painting." T. S. Eliot, the publication year of *The Waste Land*, 1922. Clem squinted above a thick exhale from his Camel, as if looking back across the years of disappointed production. Eliot had lost his stuff. On Van Gogh, the years were 1885–88, the era of *Shoes* and *The Potato Eaters*. The portraits especially "had too much paint and were not good." For Pollock, whom Clem singled out early on as the most important Abstract Expressionist, the cutoff was 1951. It amused Clem when at Pollock's 1951 show—the first not to succeed—people kept coming up to him and saying, "At last I get what you see in Pollock."

I memorized these cutoff dates, and couldn't help thinking the idea obsessed Clem because he, too, had fallen off. He attributed his nonwriting then to "writer's block." Which I took as a generic term to mean he had ceased exerting any control over his schedule. What Clem did all day was see friends, read philosophy, and visit exhibitions, with his scowling, instant discernment. He was nearing eighty.

He entered museum lobbies with a slow, pokey walk, this small bald man, as if he'd just gotten off a horse after decades in the saddle.

The last piece he'd written was about Clyfford Still. The Abstract Expressionist's best pictures had been verticals. Clem wrote the reason Still could only succeed in this format was because "he couldn't be alone with himself long enough to go horizontal." This was the kind of remark he made—an insight you just never could have come up with yourself, immediately right, and opening up more doors at the same time. And funny too. But funny in a particularly strong way. It was funny without asking you to laugh.

Once, a midwestern woman I'd met at an artist's colony wanted to meet him. She asked if I could set it up, so I brought her over. She came bearing a jar of honey, and we all spent a couple hours talking together in his study. When she left Clem said, "She's very nice, but she smiles too much, after every sentence." Of course she did. I'd noticed it, without quite gathering the energy to put it into words.

He'd also told me why he'd gone into art criticism in the first place. Early on, he'd been writing for *Partisan Review*, with its great group of New York intellectuals: Dwight Macdonald, Hannah Arendt, Irving Howe, Philip Rahv, and others. In this group Clem was just another brilliant writer. He said, "I knew I'd stand out more in the art world because there just aren't that many smart people in the field. At *Partisan Review* I had a lot of competition." So, focusing on being an art critic had been a business decision. Like his father, Clem was a very good businessman.

He told me about the Pollock–de Kooning split—that de Kooning and a lot of hangers-on thought Pollock was out of it, too awkward, too difficult, and that they'd banded together around the more accessible, movie star–like de Kooning. He called the painter Adolph Gottlieb a "pants presser." He didn't approve of Rothko killing himself in his studio and leaving a pool of blood for everyone to clean up. Rothko was high on barbiturates and actually cut an artery in his right arm with a razor blade. What painter could hurt either of his arms, the very things he created his art with?

"All that blood others were left to find and clean up," Clem said.

One time, exasperated, I finally couldn't take it anymore. I asked, "Who *did* you like, Clem?"

"I liked Pollock sober," he answered.

Pollock Sober? At first I thought it was someone's name, some obscure painter only he knew about. But no, Clem meant Pollock when he wasn't drinking. He also mentioned that he'd written a book about Jackson and Lee's relationship. He'd spent a great deal of time in the 1950s with the two of them. But ultimately he decided "it wasn't fit for publication."

As well as being brilliant he had this marvelous air of detachment. Perhaps it came from reading the *Bhagavad Gita*, which he took out of his coat pocket a few times while I was there. "Subway reading," he called it. Or maybe he had cultivated "disinterestedness" because it went along with his aesthetic theory coming out of Immanuel Kant.

He had great expressions to back up his ideas, expressions I still use. My favorite came up when Clem assigned blame for something he didn't like. He'd say, "It's the taste that permits it." This meant that if someone wanted to do something ridiculous or awful or crude or mad, that was, simply, that person's idea. For instance, Vito Acconci masturbating under the raised floorboards of Sonnabend Gallery in 1972. That was fine, and probably a fun way for Acconci to spend those hours. But it was the people who would say it was art—that was the problem. You look at a Paul Klee, you get a feeling: it sets your imagination free. You listen to Vito bringing himself off: you knew it was a blow against the squares. It was easier and simpler to have an opinion on these shock-value events. The inherent risk went away, and taste was supplanted by positions. It was the taste that *permitted* it, that went along with it, that even sponsored it. It was the taste that was to blame. The taste that couldn't, or didn't know how to, say no. Taste that was both unformed and permissive.

When something was said that he found "off," his comeback would be: "That shows you don't hang around with the right people." To do successful work, he'd whittled it down to "Just make a rule and then stick to it" or "Bear down more. The trouble is you don't bear down enough."

He even had a rule about viewing pictures. One day I bumped into him in front of a small Fra Angelico crucifixion at the Met. He was standing pretty close to it. "Every picture has its own viewing distance," he said. "It's up to the viewer to find it." You have to look at the picture to know.

And for color: "You can make any picture work if the color is good enough." He also thought that people who could see color were special, mystical, and somehow found each other. For judging art he said, you have to go picture by picture. That's the whole thing. For life too.

Clem talked a lot about "major" and "minor." When he threw those terms around, we, the painters and sculptors who knew him, were all just shaking. Everybody wanted to be major; no one could stand the thought of being minor. But a few years later I realized, "Wait, minor's not that bad. Minor's okay." You could get in; you might get into some wing at the Met. Maybe. Like Raphaelle Peale or George Bellows. Cynthia Ozick mentions the same thing in her essay "Alfred Chester's Wig." The question there was: "Will Alfred Chester even be considered minor?" One time in conversation Clem admitted, "I'd settle for being 'minor.' Hopper is minor, he's too safe."

If you started getting too specific immediately he'd say, "Don't explain." Once I was telling him what had inspired a picture, my thoughts at the time. "Cut the soundtrack," he said. "In art the only thing that matters is the result."

When I was hanging out with him from the early eighties until his death in 1994, I hadn't fallen off. I still had years ahead of me, which could be influenced by everything I'd learned from Clem. And what he said about my paintings. Maybe, like Leda in Greek mythology, "I could put on his knowledge with his power"?

DRINKS AT CLEM'S usually started around 6:00 p.m. Mostly it was just the two of us. There was a bar with whiskey, wine, and a lot of skinny Alessi thin breadsticks. I would ask for scotch on the rocks, which I thought sounded drinky. Mostly we talked about his past—the people he'd known, the art he'd seen, his opinions, even his love affairs.

One time Clem said, "It all comes down to character. In the end, it's the artist's character that makes someone a great painter." What really disturbed him was Jackson killing the woman in his car in East

Hampton. "If he wanted to kill himself, that was his business, but he didn't have to take that innocent girl down with him."

There was the night he talked about the great topic of flatness. He was constantly quoted about the "ineluctable flatness of the picture plane"—stating that for a contemporary abstract painting to succeed, to "work," it had to maintain the tension inherent in its two-dimensionality. The concept initially came out of his study of Kant. In painting, this self-aware, self-critical aspect had to do with proclaiming what it shared with no other art—*flatness*.

We were in his living room when he brought it up. Dusk was falling, and with it the light dying over the sliver of Hudson visible from his window.

"Maybe I overdid it with flatness," he said. "It wasn't that important."

I was *stunned*. It was the cornerstone of his approach to modernism, and here he was questioning what had set the course of American painting for decades.

"Really? You think that? But it's completely identified with your name. It's your main premise—Greenberg and flatness."

"Yeah, well I wish I could retract it now," he said. "Or at least make less of it. The press has made too much of it."

No doubt he could have called someone, some art critic type who would have been delighted to report this change to *Art News*, *Art in America*, or, for Christ's sake, *The New York Times*. There were others who had renounced theories in their later years. But he didn't do that.

WHEN HE VISITED my apartment I'd drive my Toyota to his place over on Central Park West and pick him up. Then we'd drive back to my apartment on West End. I liked walking with him through the brazenly mirrored lobby of my building, even though no one knew who he was.

I'd have left wine and a baguette out on a table. He'd eat the French bread and drink wine while I showed him my newest pictures. Despite his loose dentures—on the edge of falling out while he chewed—it was fun being with him.

Slowly we'd go through my large pictures—huge, really, in relation to the room's proportions—and Clem would home in on the area that had given me trouble. "The green is not working," he'd say. Or "I can tell you were trying too hard in that passage." And he'd point.

Often we'd stay sitting on my two cane chairs after his critique and read the *Times*. He was the only person I felt comfortable enough to read with.

One time he brought up the word "heterosexual." Damn, I thought. I wanted things to be neutral. I wouldn't have done anything that might jeopardize those precious times of his looking at my paintings and talking about them.

"You know," he said, "like you and me, heterosexual." Had I pursued that line of conversation we'd have had a completely different relationship. But I didn't.

CLEM WAS MARRIED, even though he and his wife didn't live together and had other relationships. But in 1991 he summoned Jenny back from LA. It meant she'd be leaving the guy she was living with. Jenny was tall, thinnish, with blond hair and a large chin—just like Clem's— almost as if they'd gotten together *because* of their chins. They'd met in the late 1950s at Bennington; she was still a student and he was visiting the college. Clem said he would always remember her baby fat from that time.

Although she did dutifully wend her way back to the eighteenth floor of 275 Central Park West, her return didn't signal a romantic move. In fact, sometimes when I was there, her boyfriend would call on the phone and she'd excuse herself to talk with him.

Not only was she not romantic about Clem, but she didn't seem to like him that much—including his habit of smoking unfiltered Camels. She went so far as to put signs up all over the apartment saying, no smoking here or smoking only in the study (a stepmother's gesture). Jenny also criticized the critic for the way he used the ice maker on their brown refrigerator door.

Once over dinner in their kitchen, Clem reminisced about how much he liked dancing. "I used to *love* to dance. It was really fun that time with Mary McCarthy." He'd also had an affair with her, which he didn't mention that evening.

Immediately Jenny chimed in: "Oh, Clem, that must have been awful. You're such a bad dancer. You must have stepped all over her toes." And then she laughed.

To let me know he found her remark inappropriate, as soon as she left the room, Clem said, "Jenny shouldn't be talking to me like that. But I'm in 'reduced circumstances' now, and there's not much I can do about it." I was impressed he was as honest with himself as he was with everyone else, that he wasn't going to gloss over her insult. That he would "call a spade a spade," to use Emerson's phrase.

A FEW YEARS LATER a symposium on Clem's work was scheduled to take place in Paris. He wanted to attend, but Jenny said no, because by then she'd lost all their money. Clem had always claimed, "Jenny is good with money. She handles the money."

Through a vague connection she'd invested their stash in some hedge fund for Broadway actors and playwrights. The number I recall, mostly from the sale of a David Smith sculpture, was $800,000. And the fund's manager turned out to have a theatrical flair of his own. By impersonating voices of his clients over the phone to bank personnel, he was able to liquidate their accounts. Then, performing a Roman Polanski, he fled the United States. At one point things got so bad at chez Greenberg that Clem started phoning relatives he hadn't seen for half a century. During this time, when I asked a random question about what he'd most like, his answer surprised me: "A million dollars."

Soon after the news broke, Clem asked me to come by. He greeted me at the door and led me into his study. We never sat in the living room when Jenny was there. She and their grown daughter were in another room. We spoke a little about the money, and then he turned to me, nodding toward the direction their voices were coming from. "You know what they're doing?" he asked. "They're cleaning a closet. That's what the goyim do when they're upset—they clean a closet."

Rather than take a trip to Paris, Clem took another sort of journey. His emphysema got worse, and he had to be hospitalized. All those unfiltered Camels. I often visited him at Lenox Hill.

One day Jenny called. "Clem is scheduled to leave the hospital today. Would you mind picking him up? I have the flu."

"Of course," I answered, and walked briskly across town, through the park, to the hospital.

Exiting the elevator on the fifth floor, at one end of a long corridor I saw ten old men seated in hospital wheelchairs. They were wearing identical blue pajamas. Greenberg happened to be among them. Even from a distance I noted his bloodshot eyes searching me out. It was I who'd come to pick him up—not the art critic Michael, who'd been his protégé; not Ken and Jules, the painters he'd touted. No, somehow it was me.

At that moment Clem was reduced to just another ailing patient in a hospital lineup.

When we got out into the November air, he said, "I love cold weather," and hailed a cab. We both slid in, and, like someone taking care of a sick person, I started to give the driver his address. Clem immediately cut me off and gave the address himself.

We entered the canopied building, and the first thing he did was pick up his mail—a famous person's mail. Shiny art exhibition announcements, art and auction-house catalogs, art magazines, all sent to him because they hoped he might attend or write up their events. Once inside his apartment he lit a cigarette and poured a scotch. It was about 1:00 p.m. Immediately Jenny leaned out of her room and said, "If you want to kill yourself, okay, but don't kill me."

The apartment looked beautiful with its large living room overlooking Central Park West and light streaming in through the windows. The phone rang, someone from *Newsweek* saying a review on his latest book was in the new edition on the newsstand. "Do you want to go to the corner and get it?" he asked. At the newsstand he bought the magazine along with two small chocolates. You could see how thrilled he was to be out of the hospital.

Back at home he read the review. He was not impressed. "I've become jaded by the attention," he said.

Then it was my turn. I mentioned the chronic pain I felt being overlooked. "Even if my paintings are great, the art world doesn't care," I said.

"Right," he answered. "You aren't a big enough name."

To change the topic he told me that at the hospital they'd asked if I was Mrs. Greenberg. "I was flattered," he said, "and didn't change their perception." Before I left he added, "Every day I feel so depressed at this time in the afternoon." His eyes looked tired.

The next and last time he was hospitalized, on the same day he was scheduled to leave I called to see how he was doing. After I said hello, he yelled into the phone, "I broke my hip, I'm finished." Once again he was right.

When I got to the hospital his leg was stretched out in traction. Covered in white plaster, Clem looked like a great papier-mâché bird. For once Jenny was there. After she left he asked me to get the nurse to remove the cast. "Tell her to get this damn thing off me," he said. I obliged. There was no way I wouldn't do what Clem asked.

The next day you could see he was more comfortable, but his wife was in a rage. She blamed me for having the traction removed. "It's because of you he doesn't have the cast on anymore, and he's not going to heal properly."

She took over: his condition, his visitors, even his calls. Whenever I arrived, she'd already be sitting there with a long yellow legal pad taking notes. Maybe she was dividing up the estate. Or, if she wasn't in the room, their daughter would be, or would have just left.

I only saw him once after that, back on Central Park West. I came early on a Tuesday and was ushered into his bedroom—a room I'd never been in before. I remember the bright yellow sheets. Which brought to mind the Hotel d'Alsace and Oscar Wilde's last yellow wallpaper.

"Hello," I said. "How are you?"

"Not that great," he answered.

"I know," I said. "This must really be a drag."

To change the topic he asked me, "What are you doing? Are you going back to Paris this summer?"

"Yeah, I'm going in a couple weeks. I'm not staying in the sixteenth this time. I'll be in the fourteenth, Montparnasse."

"Oh, that's fine. You'll like it. You should look up my friend Ann Sinclair."

"Is she French?" I asked. "It doesn't sound like a French name."

"Yes, she is," he said. "Actually she's Paul Rosenberg's granddaughter. You know the building on Seventy-Ninth where Salander-O'Reilly is? That used to be the Paul Rosenberg Gallery. He was Matisse and Picasso's dealer."

He gave me her address and phone number. Then he directed me to a closet in the bedroom.

"Go to the back, on the right. That's where I keep the maps. There's a map in there of Paris."

I fumbled around and found it.

"Take it with you," he said. "It's good on the arrondissements."

As I walked to the door of his bedroom to let myself out, he added, "I have always enjoyed your company." And that was it. Ten years of near-hero worship, over. The rest of my life ahead of me.

What kept him going through the thin eighties and the nineties was his belief that the best art would stand the test of time. Warhol would be known to future generations for what he was: a showman and impresario, *not* a great painter. But it occurs to me now that so far, Clem, himself, has *not* stood the test of time. I seem to be the only person still talking about him. It's like I'm standing on the shore, and the boat that is the art world is way, way off in the distance. No one has replaced him—not in New York and not for me. Clem is the only person I've ever known who stood for something.

THE LOUVRE

THE ONLY TIME my children and I visited the Louvre together was a few months before the turn of the century. The picture I'd always wanted to show them was Van Eyck's *The Madonna of Chancellor Rolin*. It's pretty well known through reproduction. One of those postcards that would have stunned the fifteenth century, as much a miracle as a phone. But that's never the same as seeing it in person.

The Madonna sits to the right wearing a plush red robe. The Chancellor kneels on the left, dressed in a blue, gold, and maroon robe. Although they do not seem affectionate, they do seem well matched. They face each other across a hygienic bit of distance. In the middle ground is a marvelous scene: columns, two small figures on a balcony, a bridge, and, in the very far distance, many small tan boats. This fairy-tale part seemed far from the pieties Van Eyck meant or had set out to illustrate. It made the piety seem fairy-tale too.

The work hung by itself on a back wall among its relatives and peers in the Early Netherlandish section. After looking for a few moments I felt something was missing. Then I noticed the bulb facing it was out. I showed this to the boys. There were no nearby windows to add light, so the canvas had become hard to see.

We motioned to the guard leaning against a doorway.

He kind of shrugged, then observed, "C'est généralement comme ça." Nor, while all of us waited, did he call anyone to replace the blown bulb.

On the way out—thinking I might write a letter of polite and firm complaint—I asked the museum director's name.

The woman at the desk gave me a brochure. This contained the museum's address and hours, and on the back: *Pierre Rosenberg.*

I'd been surprised she wrote it down so freely: museum directors are celebrities on the order of movie directors. I'd expected the first name would include at least one hyphen, something like Jean-Christophe or Jean-Claude. With a complicated run of nouns and syllables after, but here it was, a New York City art world name. Rosenberg, like the critic who had once come to lie on Lee Krasner's porch when I visited the famous widow of an even more famous painter.

Months later, finding the brochure among my European stuff, I sat in front of my boxy paint-stained Apple keyboard, gaze as fixed as the Chancellor's in the Van Eyck, and wrote a letter. Not hoping for a response from Monsieur Rosenberg. Simply to highlight the issue of the inattentive guard, the blown bulb, the dimmed masterpiece. For good measure, I threw in a few sentences about the constant flash-bulbs going off around the *Mona Lisa*, which made the delicate portrait nearly impossible to view, as if every Louvre visitor were staring through a silent lightning storm.

I was surprised, a few weeks later, to find an envelope with the Louvre's return address in my mailbox. One of the pleasant surprises in the unregulated space before email was opening the mailbox to find unexpected and unknown envelopes and stamps. Email abolished this pleasure, along with the marvelous, flirtatious variety of letter-writing choices: handwritten versus typed; return address or no, carefully chosen stamp or postal catch-as-catch-can. A whole world of ways to demonstrate individual elegance mashed down to sameness.

Rosenberg's letter was in French; clearly not the product of an assistant.

He assured me the Van Eyck masterpiece was now properly lit. The guard was presumably on notice for his illumination failure. As for the flashbulbs around the *Mona Lisa*, he wrote, "The Louvre is a victim of its own success."

I typed back in English to say I was glad, and next time I was in Paris I'd verify the Van Eyck's improved station in life myself.

Rosenberg had signed off with what to an American sounded gushy: "Madame, please accept the expression of my distinguished consideration." Probably in French it was just a formality. Below his expressive signature it read, "Pierre Rosenberg of the French Academy." I signed with the American "Best."

That was February. Since I'd be returning in the summer, I mentioned my itinerary to Rosenberg. He wrote back saying he was now retiring from the Louvre. He suggested we could still meet, just not at the museum. I said this sounded fine.

A WEEK AFTER my arrival I phoned. Rosenberg didn't ask, "When are you free?"—it was a slightly gloomy "When are you leaving?" The last thing any visitor wants to think of: their own dislodging from a place they've just gotten to. It seemed he used this method as a guide for making and limiting appointments. It wasn't until August that we actually met.

I consulted my Paris pratique after this call, to find his street. Rue de Vaugirard, which, like Broadway in Manhattan, is the city's longest block. Then I went about seeing everything I could. It's what painters do in cities: gorge their eyes.

This included the Louvre, days and days in a row. On the first day, I verified that the *Rolin* was now properly lit. I also checked out D'Orsay, Beaubourg, and l'Orangerie. Painters traveling are like people visiting high school friends: there are simply a certain number of faces and views you need to see. In the way that streets in SoHo had once been characterized by their inhabitants, cities become characterized by their museums and paintings. Florence is all Botticellis and Donatellos; Vienna has the cool edge of Velasquez; and Madrid, the envelope containing the marvelous Prado.

Then it was August. To distract my meeting-an-interesting-person fears—would my French be good, would the August weather make a frizzy planter out of my hair—I rushed around purchasing things:

skirt, earrings, French beauty products with their lovely solidity in the hand.

You do overestimate things while traveling. Paris clothing, in its recessive, elusive colors like taupe and mauve, simply seemed better. The drop pearl earrings outdid anything in that line at home. On the named day I walked to Rue de Vaugirard through the Jardin du Luxembourg. I had traced that route with my finger many times that summer, and easily found Pierre's number 60 printed on a big blue door. How would the man who had once overseen a whole museum, the world's great museum, live?

I opened that blue door, punched in the code Rosenberg had given me on the steel panel keyboard. Having that building code seemed oddly intimate. That took me to an interior courtyard with gardens. From the street you would never have anticipated the gardens existed. It was like that strange world contained in the center of the Van Eyck. After a moment I found the apartment number. And then the suspense, once you'd pressed the doorbell, having no idea what the person who comes to the door will look like. What their presence will *feel* like. It's the same as stepping into a new museum for the first time, knowing only something good awaits you, but not knowing the taste of the memories the visit will leave you with. Memories always have a taste you can never guess at in advance—a combination of the things you saw, the way they made you feel, the connected things this made you think of, your interest in returning; all the flavors a memory can take, the compound of these impressions and ambitions.

There stood Monsieur Rosenberg of the French Academy. Gray hair that puffed out on either side of a bald head, like the wisp of wings on the child angels in a Raphael. Hard, canny face, blue eyes. Immediately I thought of a cat.

He was wearing a light-colored shirt, no tie, and his pants seemed weirdly loose. Around his neck he did sport a red scarf. We said our hellos and he led me past several large rooms into what looked like a study. There was nobody else around in the whole big, breezy place.

We talked mostly about Poussin. Rosenberg was one of that artist's foremost scholars. If someone had to validate a Poussin, they'd reach out to him. We also spoke about Chardin. It turned out Pierre had organized a major Chardin retrospective that had traveled to Manhattan. I'd seen it four times—so, in a way, I had already traveled a little in Rosenberg's imagination, I'd already been his visual guest. The conversation was conducted in English. He sat at his desk—as I had when I first wrote him about the light bulb. I sat in a chair facing him as if this were an academic office hour or a job interview.

Then he brought up retirement. "You probably think I'm sixty-five," he said, "because retirement in the US comes without exception at that age. But in France this same retiring age is sixty-two." He clearly wanted me to know about these two years of extra youth. The second most personal thing he mentioned was about being married to someone named Beatrice, who apparently lived elsewhere in Paris. Later I learned she was a Rothschild—and not a distant Rothschild, but part of the core family group with "de" in front of her name. The government had officially granted this *de* to her ancestors in the 1820s. I'd once had a close American friend who was very rich in this same ancient way, so this data put me at ease: as if my life had certain patterns and I was somehow pleasantly returning to them.

After a couple of hours, he signaled it was time for me to leave. Then I was outside, in the pleasant heat of this neighborhood of Paris, with its leaf shadows and birds who either knew or didn't that, city-wise, they really had it made, and the feel of my new blouse sticking lightly to my back. The question as I clicked down Rue de Vaugirard was whether I had failed the academic interview. Hard to say.

A few more blocks and the question changed: Had the interview been for the position of lover? Again, hard to say. Maybe he didn't have lovers? With the Rothschild legacy staring down perhaps I wasn't even a viable candidate? Or something in the by-laws for a family that venerable forbade *any* lighthearted infidelity.

On my end there had been no specific agenda either. I'm a painter. Beyond my curiosity about how this former director lived, I would've settled, indeed been happier, with his introduction to a French art dealer or some rich French collectors.

THREE SUMMERS LATER, in 2003, I painted in the tenth arrondissement. The apartment had many rooms and a large terrace. The huge marble staircases dated from 1640. Moroccans sat outside in front of open cars, selling delicious mangoes from cartons. Rosenberg and I met one late afternoon in August.

It was the hottest August in decades—day after day peaked above 40 degrees Celsius. Many people died. Because it was August the French dignitaries were all at the beach and very few bothered to return and oversee this crisis. Some afternoons, as the temperature slammed sweat from my forehead and I felt a surge of blood when I turned too quickly, I realized I too could die from the heat. But I didn't want to leave without seeing Rosenberg.

Instead, every morning I stood on my lovely terrace in the unmoving air. The view was less fairy-tale than the view in that Van Eyck that had brought me in touch with Rosenberg, but it was romantic to me. It had the romance of novelty, of things you let affect you, rather than the things you see every day and have no say about changing. The Paris view, in a way nothing in New York had been since SoHo, had the prized quality of being my own idea. Then I'd go back inside. It was said the heat wave was coming from Africa. Even that, the source of a heat wave, could seem in its deadly way enchanting.

Only a handful of city places even had air conditioning. Some days I sought refuge in the Deux Magots café. To avoid the evening heat, I'd follow and drift among the crowd on Rue de Faubourg Saint-Martin toward the Luxembourg Garden. Everyone sweating and suffering in a kind of numerous, slowly moving silence. Sometimes I thought the crowds might break into "La Marseillaise" like survivors of some

World War II battle in a patriotic French movie. At night I slept next to an open window in the kitchen. From my cold spot on the floor tile I could see the moon shining brightly over oddly shaped Parisian roofs.

Pierre, I imagined, was riding out the emergency in more elegant surroundings. I pictured a servant fetching one of those slightly skinny and undersize Parisian glasses and passing it to the director on a small lacey silver tray.

Pierre had written that I should call in August, but still I was surprised to find him in Paris enduring the deadly heat wave. On the phone, with a dry chuckle he mentioned staying in during the day with the shades drawn, venturing out only at night. I decided against telling him about my sleeping spot on the floor, but I wondered if we'd ever moved in the same murmuring, swaying crowds on those strange, tranced evenings. We arranged to see each other again at Vaugirard two days later.

Another way to reach his sixth-arrondissement apartment was through Saint-Sulpice, with its church that houses Delacroix's wonderful, refreshing frescoes. Around the square were yellow leaves that had prematurely fallen on the pavement: casualties of the emergency. The leaves still on the trees were crinkly as if it were late autumn.

Heat wave or no, Pierre greeted me at the door wearing his red scarf. He whisked me past rooms where I imagined his painting collection waited and back to the study with his desk and the chair for me beside it. There was one small difference—someone appeared with orange juice and cookies on a silver tray, as if I had somehow imagined that tray into existence. In my fantasy, though, Pierre's drink had been a sort of fortifying cocktail. I had a strange thought then: the Chancellor Rolin painting had brought me and this man into some tenuous connection, and we were sitting the same way the sitters in that painting did. Pierre at a workspace, me across from him. It was like a strange trick the Louvre was playing on us both.

America had recently invaded the Middle East and we discussed potential outcomes, speculated what might happen. Pierre said the Americans had made a big mistake: France had been ruined for years because the Algerian War had ultimately drained her and accomplished nothing. And that was the path America had now embarked on. What he said seemed wise and European. Of the heat, Pierre said that he'd splurged and bought a humidifier. I had the impression that since it would betray French values, an air conditioner was out of the question. When it was time to leave I found myself mildly disappointed.

Again I reviewed everything on the walk home, which had the same swaying crowds, the same arms held away from the slow-moving bodies to allow what breeze there was access to the human trunk. The only change now, I thought, was another chapter in my connection to this man Rosenberg. Yet, other than time advancing—Americans would have now forced Pierre to retire—nothing had changed since the first visit. It was as if the parameters had been permanently fixed, as iron as the grating that protects people on the balconies of the city from a fall into something they cannot control.

The next day I called Air France and moved my departure up, and it was on the airplane, having escaped the burning city, that I truly appreciated the great American innovation of personal air conditioning. This made me grateful for Pierre. As if weirdly the whole connection had been designed to make me appreciate what was especially admirable about the world I was really from.

IT WAS FOUR YEARS LATER when I saw Pierre again. An Italian friend had offered me his Venice apartment. No strings attached. Although, as a gift I did leave Mino a small painting. My whole life, I've found ways to pay for things with paintings. There are many difficulties to being an artist but there is this advantage.

Venice was the most beautiful city.

It was as if Pierre had somehow gotten mixed into my ideas of travel: as if I would always be the woman in the Chancellor Rolin painting, staring at the Chancellor, that in the middle would be this scene of boats and water, and each time I left America my thoughts would be trained to return to him.

A few days after my arrival I recalled that Pierre had gone on in some detail about an apartment he had in Venice. We'd made the jump to email, the correspondence conducted exclusively in English. No more foreign stamps, no more comparisons of handwriting. And the loss of sexiness—no holding the paper and thinking the other person who was part of your various imaginings had once touched it.

I emailed Pierre to say I was in Venice. He wrote back with the phone number. Once again Pierre asked my departure date. By now, I had learned: I bumped up my plans, claimed to be leaving three days later. There was a pause.

He asked if I knew the Vaporetto stop Giglio. We arranged to meet in the park there at noon, after which we'd have lunch at his apartment. I pictured a kind of floor-through, like the very lovely one I was staying in.

Not knowing how long it would take, I arrived early and had to find a place to hide out, until I could coolly emerge around 12:10. There was a Da Vinci exhibition in a church on the square, and when I came out Pierre was sitting on a bench in the bright noonday sun, the red scarf intact. I realized I had never seen him outdoors.

We started walking. Walking and walking, in the pink sloshy light, past the little green shrubs and pastel-colored houses. Venice, that strange city of marble angles. This was so much like the Van Eyck painting with its burned-out bulb at the Louvre: marble and canals. Finally, after what seemed like half an hour he led me up some wooden stairs. They weren't ordinary, but wide and polished, what you imagined might lead you up to a palace.

And, sure enough, when he opened the door with his huge iron key, the two of us were, in fact, inside a palace. Pierre and Beatrice's palazzo, on the Grand Canal—or maybe it was just Beatrice's? Or her family's? Once again, she was absent.

Pierre gave me a tour. "Chopin composed in this room when he was extremely ill," he said with a gesture. "James finished *The Wings of the Dove* in that room." The place was dripping with history. Pierre even took me out onto the roof where you could see all of Venice. Strange how people seemed so integral to Paris, but in Venice they had the feel of an illusion, or of figures added to a Renaissance sketch only for the benefit of the two-point perspective. I'd never been to a city where people felt so temporary and unnecessary. Right across the canal was the museum that housed François Pinault's contemporary art collection. It was a collection nobody on my side of the art world respected. The dated sculpture outside was made of tin cans and other metal objects soldered together. Pinault's offerings—they had no beauty—defiled the beautiful palazzo and the Grand Canal.

Pierre and I were served lunch in the dining room beside the water. There we were, sitting on antique wooden chairs, with the water outside the windows, some boats scattered on the surface. The serving woman whispered something to Pierre in Italian. Leaning over he asked me, "Is it too cold for you with the window open? Sofia thinks you might be enduring a draft?" Whatever I'd almost thought of just then was gone.

I was touched. First the conversation was about coffee. When I mentioned Colombian coffee—which I bought and poured into a dusty grinding machine at Whole Foods—he scrunched up his face. "Colombian is a lesser beverage. *Nothing* beats Italian espresso." He was one of those people, I realized, who had fallen into a state of reverence, of fandom, toward their own life. He asked what I'd been doing since my arrival. "Oh, I just saw the Sargent 'Paintings in Venice.'" It had been on, and it was fascinating to see an American painter here. I wondered if his impressions would somehow match mine: the paintings weren't great but Sargent seemed to feel the nonnecessity of people in his images. "Why would you bother with that?" Pierre asked with a face.

His response was surprising since I hadn't implied Sargent was in my top ten list or anything. And I couldn't think of a way to express what had interested me: the buildings and the water being the permanent things, as they were in Guardi's and Monet's about the city. Our conversation was turning out far less successful than the beautifully served lunch in the wood-ceilinged room. Still, when the meal ended I did not want to leave.

In an enormous vestibule I saw, leaning on a little table easel, a small painting around the size of a notebook page. It was clearly of Velazquez's *Las Meninas*. I asked, "Who did the small study?" And was flummoxed when Pierre looked at me for a moment and then answered, "Oh, that's by Sargent."

I COULD END THIS STORY HERE. But a few years later Pierre organized an exhibition of Poussin's late nature paintings in New York at the Met. I was excited to find the invitation from him to the opening in my mailbox. A real letter again.

I arrived at the museum in my favorite black outfit—silk pants, cashmere turtleneck—and was greeted by mostly French people. Men with chicly long hair in perfectly tailored suits. Women who were neither overstated nor understated, but who just stated perfectly what it was they were, what age and status they had. This fittingness, this tact, this visual economy, may be what is so entrancing to Americans about the French. Americans who ad-lib, and those who overdo and underdo everything. Everyone was tremendously charming like a fantasy party surrounded and supervised by great paintings. The presence of good art does seem to make people better. I knew no one and looked for Pierre.

I found him in front of *Blind Orion Searching for the Rising Sun*. For once, no red scarf. He gave me a very dry peck on the cheek and took me aside. "My wife isn't here," he said. He looked anxious. "She hasn't shown up yet."

I thought, *Why is he confiding in me?* He had never once spoken about his wife's schedule. She had orbited our meetings and discussions with no more effect upon them than the moon, which was also there and far away, and also went without mention. "I'm not even sure she's going to be in attendance this evening," he continued. Suddenly this man seemed his own age, far from home, and a little vulnerable. When you always see someone in their home, you have no idea how they'll fare as a traveler.

"Take a deep breath," I advised. "She'll be here soon."

In honor of Pierre's exhibition many of his friends had flown in from Paris. He introduced me. All these attractive men smiling and joking. This is what it might have felt like, to be the woman attached to this man.

Twenty minutes later Pierre returned as if I'd become his emergency contact, or his sponsor. "She is still not in attendance," he said.

Then I noticed a tall woman wearing an elegant gown and sensible shoes. "I think she's there," I said, pointing, then watched as Pierre walked toward her. I wondered if she'd come late to upstage him, or simply to make him nervous. I had been unmarried for a long time, and had forgotten the gestures of rebellion and advantage that marriage is composed of.

Philip de Montebello, the Met's director, was among the guests. Although we'd never met he crossed to where I stood and for some reason we pretended to know each other. "How are you?" he said. "It's been a while." Then the director leaned over and kissed my cheek.

We arranged for Beatrice and Pierre to visit my studio the following evening. There was light snow, but they appeared at my studio on time just the same. I served French wine I thought might be passable for someone used to Lafite Rothschild—a famous vintage named for one's own family—and we began the usual steps of small talk that precede a studio visit. This tends to be about what shows you've recently seen. But it's really a way of both parties adapting each other to their own particular conversational and visual rhythms, a mutual charming. Although totally French and a baroness to boot, Beatrice spoke English in a deep voice without accent.

And she had no idea who I was. "How do you know Pierre?" she finally asked.

Their clothes seemed to match. Since I was concentrated on faces, what I mostly saw was their neckwear. She wore a bright red scarf. Pierre wore a burgundy scarf trimmed in blue and gold. I discussed the Van Eyck, the unconcerned guard, how her husband had solved things with a new bulb. His remark about the storms of tourist lightning around the famous Da Vinci portrait. There was a pause. "I don't understand. Have you visited our apartment?" she slowly asked.

I wasn't prepared enough for directness to have a lie ready. Normally I need preparation of a few seconds to say something untruthful. When push comes to shove, I will reply automatically with the truth. I said I had been there.

Pierre nervously asked to see some paintings. My assistant Shala and I pulled out a few of my later works, large paintings with muted color. Pierre offered that one or two had what he called Poussin color. And I admired that. I had looked at Poussin a lot after knowing this was his specialty. He was right to see it. It was a flash of how gifted he must have been. That blue, ochre, and khaki green combination was from the French painter's palette. When Beatrice mentioned she collected contemporary prints my assistant showed a few of my monotypes. Beatrice chose one that had a price tag laughably under her budget: $1,800. "I'll take that," she said firmly, and wrote out her check on the spot. On a separate paper she began to write her Paris address for me to send it to, then stopped. "But of course you already know our address." We all got up and walked to the door.

The print was sent to the house with the gardens and the many dark rooms. I never saw either of them again.

ROGER LEVY

HIS NAME WAS ROGER LEVY. I heard it first from Basel Fritz, a Yale Art School type I was having a show with. Fritz wrote art reviews for *The New Yorker*. But, like so many reviewers, he was also a painter. These critic-painters wore two hats, and consequently had "too much on their plates." It was a constant whirl of alternating haberdashery and china, the two New York clichés of that moment, and even later. It was embarrassing to hear a friend use them. But what could you do?

Fritz had just finished hanging his series of paintings—friends at cocktail parties holding wineglasses—in the gallery's project room. It was a small side space off the main gallery, where my work was to be installed later that month. Dorothy Zapruder's gallery was not a ground-floor space. And not on one of the core six blocks of the Chelsea art world either. This meant less foot traffic. With only two·people working there, one of whom was the owner who sometimes doubled as receptionist, it wasn't close to being a top-tier gallery. But that's where you find yourself sometimes.

My thinking then was: better than nothing. But there were times I wasn't so sure. At the end of the day's hang Basel and I left together. He mentioned someone named Roger Levy, who was throwing him a party at this brownstone on West Seventy-Fourth Street. He asked if I wanted to come. I thought, *So there are still rich guys with brownstones who throw parties after openings.* Naively, I'd assumed this New York

phenomenon had ended in the eighties when I stopped paying attention, the same way that after high school I thought teenagers stopped
staying up all night making out.

I didn't accept the invitation. But the name had stayed with me. That
someone named Levy, whom I didn't know, had a few years before
reviewed a museum exhibition I was in and *not* mentioned my work.
It's the kind of thing a painter never forgets.

A few weeks later I was invited to another party at Levy's, and this
time I accepted.

He didn't live in a brownstone actually. It was a loft and on the Lower
East Side of New York. I knew this area well because I went there periodically to buy ribbon, which I used in place of frames on the sides of
my pictures.

With reddish hair and a drink in hand, he had become a figure in
one of his friend's pictures. Roger Levy was welcoming guests when
I arrived. The walls of his home were lined with small, unresolved
pictures—students' work. As I was leaving he asked for my card and
nodded in recognition when he saw my name.

Let me say what I mean by unresolved—it's when nothing works
together—you could remove any part of the painting and it wouldn't
make a difference.

Another of his hats, I learned, was that he ran the noncommercial
Clocktower Gallery, which put on shows that sometimes got reviewed
in *The New York Times*. About a month later he sent me an email invitation to their next opening. I decided to attend. As we spoke his eyes
kept darting around the room, as if he was looking for who else might
be available to speak with. I thought it wasn't cool—though I did like
his Scots accent—and certainly not in line with the unwritten code
for art openings. What you wanted to project was rapt attention to the
person you were speaking with, since this reflected well on your own
self-esteem.

I asked, "Why are you looking around the room while we're talking?"

"Am I?" he said, then charmingly blushed at being called on it. I've always preferred men who like being called on stuff. He mumbled something that I didn't quite get because (a) my hearing was poor; and (b) his accent, although commanding, dropped at the second half of every sentence. When I did understand what he said I noticed that everything sounded ten percent better than it would have in American English.

A few months later another work of mine was hanging in Dorothy Zapruder's viewing room, a space that was supposed to promote sales but hardly ever did. Roger emailed me. "I just saw your picture at Zapruder, and it's a real masterpiece. The way you used those subtle grays, very Manet." As usual, with the slightest word of encouragement I overreacted. *He totally gets my work*, I thought.

Through emails—the medium he seemed happiest in—we struck up a correspondence.

The color of his size-ten font was gray. When I sent out a mass mailing about my new website he wrote back, "It is as spare and elegant as you." It took twenty emails to get to the next step.

The studio visit: Roger first suggested the possibility of one but left specifics vague. The whole thing had the same gray effect as his font. One Saturday morning the phone rang. "Hi, it's Roger Levy," he said. "I'm going to a couple of galleries in your building and wondered if I could come by to see your work." When I asked how soon his voice had a shrug in it. "An hour or two?"

"Sure." I tried to sound nonchalant while I looked around the totally disheveled space. It would have to be cleaned up without an assistant in an hour. But the truth is, had I received the call in the hospital, immobilized and snorkeled to an IV, I'd have unplugged my IV and made it to the studio on time. Critics made me see neon lights. The field was so competitive, anything a critic might write about your work could help. After hanging up, I raced around frantically, collecting Q-tips, jars, lids, and other debris. I vacuumed a paint-covered rug that ran the length of the room, touched up walls with white paint, then unwrapped the large pictures I was going to show him. When he knocked on the door an hour later, wearing a fedora, the room was passable. Cleaning has the nice side effect of focusing you.

He looked at the first picture intensely and made some sharp critical remark that reflected well on his Slade Art School background. When I put up the second, he made another equally astute comment. We went through the whole group, picture by picture. After the viewing he even knew to take a tour around the room, remarking on my postcards, photographs, and favorite quotes hanging on the wall. For example, *Do not act as if you had a thousand years to live. The inescapable is hanging over your head. While you have life in you, while you still can, make yourself good.* Marcus Aurelius. Over my desk was a picture of me as a student in the Music Room at Cornell, about which he remarked, "So you were always beautiful."

A total success, I thought after he left. I was about twenty minutes into the arduous task of rewrapping—staple gun, clamp, and plastic in hand—when there was a knock on the door. I wondered, *What delivery person could possibly be coming at three o'clock on a Saturday afternoon?*

It wasn't a delivery. It was a re-hatted Roger standing in the doorway. Had he left something?

There's a certain ritual to the New York studio visit—almost like a gourmet meal, or the absolutely traditional Japanese tea service. First there are light opening remarks (appetizers), then the properly timed move to the work (plates cleared, main course), accompanying insights (side salad), and clarifications (sorbet) followed by subtle name-dropping (seasoning), and finally the friendly (but not too friendly) departure (dessert for the table) that clearly asks for and promises *nothing.* Returning is not in the script.

"Wow, Roger, it's you," I said.

"Actually, I was having such a good time I wanted to hang out some more. Want to come round to some galleries with me now? I'm hitting a few in Chelsea, and then the slog to East Seventy-Ninth Street."

"Sure," I said, switching gears. Gallery-hopping right then seemed a preferable alternative to rewrapping all ten paintings myself. If I waited until Monday I could call the young woman who sometimes worked for me.

Then, too, as a female painter it was hard to know exactly *what* was being offered. Did Roger Levy really like my work? Was he possibly considering writing something, or did he want to sleep with me?

Making the rounds with Roger turned out to be fun. Stylish people who worked in galleries and the gallerists themselves were very attentive (art critics being third in their hierarchy of important people, after only museum panjandrums and collectors). We saw a couple of shows, then stopped for coffee at the little shop on Seventy-Ninth and Madison. He told me he'd left Scotland two years before. His parents, he said, had moved to Israel.

That was all prelude. Followed by his daily gray emails in which he discussed Israel and the Jews (for some reason unclear to me—not having his more serious Jewish background—I shared his passion on this topic). All Jews, I guess, have an interest in it: the lonely fact of belonging to a tiny group. How could this *not* be interesting? We also did a few Friday nights not in shul but at another kind of temple, the Frick Museum.

In July I went to Paris, to an empty apartment loaned to me by a friend. In a certain kind of sly movie you'd see me locking and delighting one square room in New York and instantly unlocking and lighting a similar square room in Paris. I threw myself into the usual stuff. Full of ambition when I returned to New York, I sent out a self-promoting group email about a video interview I'd given for a documentary about Morris Louis. Our work had always been somewhat similar so that in a lecture about my painting in Italy I heard I was described as a romantic interest, which was absurd, as I'd never met him. Roger must have had a slow July because he jumped at this information. He asked if he could come by to see the film. He arrived at my apartment wearing Bermuda shorts. His legs were untanned, and he wore Greek sandals that showed off his perfect toes. When I complimented them Roger said, "In fact, there's a flaw on one toe that my mother pointed out so they're not really perfect."

"So you have a family background in criticism," I said.

After a few pokes of the DVD in the MacBook slot we were able to watch the documentary about Morris Louis. I was pleased with my performance: there'd been no chance to screen the footage beforehand and this was my first viewing. Talking about the originality of Louis's work I had said, "What Louis invented, in my opinion, is so specific and so profound, and comes so much out of him, that no one but he could achieve the paintings. No one could do a Louis, but Louis." It was nice to see a clip, and this one was okay. I thought I looked somehow sexy in the footage, the way I like to arrange myself to look in the mirror.

Roger didn't get up to leave, but stayed seated on the couch. Unpredictably he launched into the oral history of his adolescence, his first high school year in a posh and lonely Scottish boarding school. The school had catered deliberately to Christians. It was part of their four-hundred-year tradition. There had been active resistance among the handful of Jewish boys: "You don't have to kneel," one whispered to him in chapel, "just because it's what the goyim do." He talked about his college poetry writing (the poems, he claimed, had been stolen from his room and then published in the school's magazine). And about stalking the campus beauty, the police ringing his door and demanding he desist. This pleased me: I have often noticed that any time a man tells you of other romances—even unhappy ones, even utter failures—it's a kind of declaration of intent, and a reminder of those particular body parts. It's a way of introducing them into the conversation, the negotiation for the next meeting that so much of a social encounter is. The portrait he drew was of a somewhat disturbed and frequently rejected young man, and I wondered why he had been so honest. I did not consider that he was so deep in self-interest that he had lost that necessary talent, being able to intuit how things he said would sound to others.

Then I started getting distracted by a reddish vertical crease in the middle of his forehead. This looked like eczema. It kept moving up and down as the Roger Levy facial expressions changed. And I found it hard not to stare.

Yes, the critic thing was a plus. And the noncommercial Clocktower Gallery would be a nice place to exhibit—I had already calculated how many of my big canvases would fit there. But I decided not to encourage this slightly overweight and intelligent but sad and awkward man. That part of a person that's independent, that hangs back and coolly calculates advantages and odds, told me that getting involved with Roger—who if I bothered to check was quite a bit younger than me—would be a mistake.

The art world takes odd people—fills them with ambition and desires to ride waves of interest into positions of further influence and greater power. One of the things a consuming profession like art does is separate you from the normal world of feelings and valuations. In art it's goal first and everything subordinate after. And by showing me his vulnerabilities, on this strange and pregnant day, Roger told me he wasn't truly outfitted for our world. And the solaces we might have offered each other, through the codes of that world, became impossible.

ALONE IN A ROOM

IT'S AROUND 9:30 and I'm walking up Tenth Avenue to my studio on West Twenty-Sixth. The building that houses it started out as a book-binding firm by the name of Wolff, which is still printed in stone over the first set of front doors. In fact, in the 1950s and '60s, the whole block between Tenth and Eleventh was given over to bookbinding. The second entrance, the one I take, is in the middle of the block and has big glass doors. They lead into a nondescript lobby where there's a small elevator, the slowest in Chelsea. Khan sits patiently inside wait-ing for the next passenger. He takes me up to ten.

My big, high-ceilinged studio at the end of a long corridor faces south. Entering it the first thing I experience is silence. (Especially in contrast to the noise I just heard walking over.) The second is privacy. Because my name is on the door, no one can enter unless invited. Nor is the large room part of something else—a house, a school, an apart-ment. It's only for me to work in. A moment of great happiness in my later life was pasting the letters of my name onto the door of room 1011. They're still there, exactly where I put them in 1998.

The room is white. At the far end there is a wooden painting rack where all my A-level pictures are kept. Everything I need to work—paint, sponges, jars, cans, brushes—is on a large wooden table just where I left them yesterday.

It's said that for years Giacometti kept things stationary in his Paris studio—which he called "the prettiest and humblest of all"—because anything moved might hinder his ability to make connections. No one was even allowed to dust. Over time my space has evolved into a studio that represents me. Photographs, postcards, and little drawings hang along one wall: my ancestors dating back to 1880; shots of my mother and father at different ages; friends and mentors; our old house; and postcards of the paintings I've seen and loved. Sometimes I add to these, but not too often.

The first thing I do is take off my street clothes—replacing them with paint-splattered jeans and a similarly covered shirt, plus paint-encrusted tennis shoes. Those early twentieth-century photographs that show a suited—always male—painter sitting at an easel have to be staged. Even in a smock no one could stay that neat.

If my glass palette—white paper is kept under it so mixed colors can be seen against white—wasn't cleaned yesterday, I scrape it with a new single-edge razor blade. Next, I do a brush check, making sure all paint residue has been removed. If not, I wash the brushes again in a slop sink behind the painting rack. Then I put on blue plastic gloves and start.

The last canvas I worked on is turned facing the wall. I carry the picture over to some old white gallon cans on the floor, place it on them, and lean it against the wall. Then I step back and look. When I left yesterday it seemed terrific—the fruit of a whole day's work. Now it's not holding up. Is it the morning light?

I don't remember exactly why it looked successful to me before. But for painters this delusional phase is a common occurrence. To be enthusiastic and positive—perhaps in order to paint at all—one needs to get carried away. But a good night's sleep brings objectivity, and the next day I can actually *see* the picture. Matisse said, "Enter the painting at its weakest link." Easy. I look for the color that's not working and start there.

Oil paint comes in shiny tubes that are squeezed like toothpaste until nothing is left inside. Larger-than-life-size canvases like mine require lots of tubes. White, which is used for mixing, comes king-size. Because oil paint is inherently viscous, half my time is spent mixing it to a smooth consistency.

I squirt some colors onto my palette and start blending them with a palette knife. After I get a good mixture it's scooped into a pint-size plastic delicatessen container and then mixed with a big wooden spoon—the same type Willem de Kooning showed me in his Springs studio—until the color is the consistency of light cream.

I test this on my canvas, just a tiny dab to see if it works in context. The thing is to get the different colors carrying their own loads. (You don't want a color overwhelming its neighbors.) If the mixture doesn't pass muster, I add a little of this, a little of that, then dab it onto the canvas again. Usually there are several attempts before I'm ready to brush the new color on, for which I use a three-inch pig hair brush. The goal is a smooth, uninflected surface that doesn't show any "hand"—like early Netherlandish painting.

Again, I step back to look. All day—back and forth—*the painter's dance.*

Throughout the process there's always the problem of *seeing.* It's tied up with everything you know and all about taste. What I've learned is that no one sees the same. The repository of images in our brains since birth influences our responses to all visual stimuli. (An easy example: if you know Cubism, an African mask will look more familiar to you than if you don't.)

Different moods influence how we see. Which is accurate—the first, fresh view or the later, knowing one? Another question: Is the eye a muscle that you can develop over time or simply a stable organ that depends on the brain's interpretation? My eye doctor confirmed the latter, explaining that once a signal reaches the visual cortex it is translated by the brain to create an image.

It's about seeing and judging (what Kant called "judgments of taste"). Jackson Pollock tried to break out of judging entirely by painting on the floor. He said,

On the floor I am more at ease. I feel nearer, more part of the painting, since this way I can walk around it, work from the four sides and
literally be in the painting.

But then in the end he sought judgment from his wife, Lee Krasner.
His question to her wasn't "Is it good?" but "Is it a painting?"

Once I've put the colors on, because it's abstract I can turn the painting in any direction. Now I go one rotation to the right. Like a kaleido-
scope, the picture looks different in each orientation. I never decide
which side is the top until the picture is finished. And sometimes even
years later I might change it. Since art is all about result, the direction
the painting works best in is the right one.

I reach for my Japanese Nichiban tape. It's translucent and comes in
quarter-inch, half-inch, and one-inch rolls. It doesn't stick to the paint
surface the way other tapes do. New York Central was the only store in
Manhattan that carried it, but since they closed two years ago I've had
to import it from Japan. I run tape along one edge. Then, to protect it,
I cover the canvas near where I'm going to apply fresh paint with strips
of Bounty paper towel. Again, I drag the paint-laden brush over a section of canvas. Then I reach for my box of skinny Q-tips. They're not
sold in pharmacies but come from a medical-supply factory in Maine.
I first saw them in the fifth-floor conservation studio at the Morgan
Library. The conservator told me where I could buy them. Each Q-tip
has a long, thin wooden handle with a cotton swab on its end. I use
this to blur the edge I just painted.

My back is starting to hurt so I lie down on a foam roller. There's
no clock in the studio, but when it feels like about ten minutes have
passed I get up, wash my hands and brushes, and continue.

Enough on the first picture, I think. Sometimes I actually put my
right hand up like a traffic cop and say out loud, "Enough, Pat, stop."
The hardest thing in abstraction is knowing when to stop. When is
it enough, and when is it too much? The kind of questions Aristotle
asked about everything: too much, too little, the right amount? Even

in ancient Rome, Pliny the Elder complimented artists "who kn[e]w when to take their hand from the picture."

If I go too far, there's always a risk of losing it. In writing you can go back to an earlier draft. Not so in painting, where *each layer obliterates the one underneath.*

So I turn that canvas to the wall and grab a smaller one. It fits flat on my forty-eight-inch table. To see it, I sit down on the top of a six-foot ladder. The color looks a little tepid, so I climb back down and start mixing Cadmium Red Medium and Titanium White with a touch of Ivory Black. Then I dab that onto the canvas where it might go and climb back up to look down again.

All these supplies—colors, tape, brushes, sponges, tape measures, Q-tips—are essential. I can't paint if I'm missing any one of them because they're not interchangeable. If I think a color must be middle red, I need *that* medium shade of red. If it has to be an off-green, I need Terre Verte. It's said that Picasso, when he was painting in Montmartre, would use green if he didn't have red. I can't do that. For me colors are like people.

I don't write down the mixtures either, the way the color guru Josef Albers did (recipes neatly written on the backs of his masonite panels). I tried doing that, but the pieces of paper fell on the floor or got spilled on. Then, too, how could I characterize the amount "a little"? So I *remember* the mixtures. That's why I keep working on the same canvases pretty consistently. During a particular time there's a familiarity I develop with each palette that makes it sort of a color diary.

Sometimes people bring me technical books about color. I like the ones that are historical: how pigments were developed in a given century, what the meanings of colors were in different cultures. The ones that encourage the use of a color wheel are of less interest.

Paul Klee said, "Color and I are one. I am a painter." Later Hans Hofmann wrote that successful paintings have their own "color-worlds." Cézanne's late landscapes of Mont Sainte-Victoire have that—a blue/green/ochre/rust quality that transcends words.

Like numbers, colors are infinite. One could spend her whole life breaking down any one color and never come to its end. The names of colors, though, are arbitrary—like the rose, they could be called "by any other name" and remain the same. It might take four ups and downs on the ladder to finally get a red that "clicks," which I then paint on the canvas. That's all, and the painting is turned face-to-the-wall to look at tomorrow.

Time for lunch. Even with plastic gloves on, my hands are dirty because I keep taking them off. On a bathroom trip I notice paint on my face, mostly blue. I wash it off with soap and water. Lead poisoning, which I once had, can come from skin absorbing oil paint.

In 1998, when I moved in, there was a big view of the Hudson, but over the years construction has whittled it down. Still, on the remaining sliver of river, I might see a boat or two glide by.

I'm feeling calmer than when I arrived—more in tune with myself. Through a sort of alchemy that turns base metals into gold, my tension and anxiety have oozed into the pictures. With the exception of noise, not much can bother me now. But there's a lot of that around, constant drilling, sawing, beeping, hammering. It can start up at any moment.

I keep working until it is about four in the afternoon. The studio is a mess, stuff has fallen to the floor, and there's a lot of soiled paper towel everywhere. Used skinny Q-tips lie around like wooden pickup sticks. I wash my brushes again and scrape the glass palette clean for the last time. Then I sit down for a moment with my legs up on the desk. Suddenly it feels claustrophobic in the studio. My two best moments are entering in the morning and leaving in the late afternoon.

OIL AND STEEL

EVERYONE CALLED HIM DICK. Even without a Welsh accent, he managed to sound like Dylan Thomas. Possibly this was the result of an early year at radio announcer's school. Or maybe great voices simply ran in his family. Dick's uncle had been an opera singer.

Dick was considered ethereal by many people in the art world. It was a surprise to discover he thought like a real estate developer. This was the kind of information that never actually made it to the public, where his image remained rumpled clothing, eccentric habits, and charm. That something beautiful in his refined looks.

Because of this charisma, people tended to project lofty ideas onto Dick. But in addition to painting, poetry, and music, he was extremely interested in money. People accused him of a lack of interest in money only because he had failed to really accumulate any.

I remember telling him about the homes once owned by my grandparents in Manhattan Beach, Brooklyn: no-frills investment properties for working men and their families. It had been part of an involved anecdote about me at age five. But instead of focusing on that Dick asked, "What happened to the bungalows?"

When I told him my landlord had just bought me out of a rent-stabilized apartment for fifty thousand dollars—I used this to get a studio back, to get my life back, and it's the studio I still have now—Dick wondered whether I should have held out for seventy-five.

And still his public image remained unsullied by trade. Which was funny, if you thought about it: Dick's day job, as it had been since the sixties, was buying and selling art.

WE MET WHEN he visited my sooty basement studio on East Eighty-Eighth Street. I was twenty-seven and married. He was forty. Dick was so in then that just about the coolest thing you could say was, "Dick Bellamy is coming to my studio." Right before we met, he'd been the director of the Green Gallery, which belonged—before they split up, each taking half the paintings with them—to the taxicab millionaires Robert and Ethel Scull. If you live in New York City you know Ethel Scull. She is the Warhol portrait at the Whitney Museum, which for half a century visitors have habitually mistaken for Jacqueline Onassis. Yellow cabs, not White Houses: but rich in one place blurs and eventually comes to look like rich in some other place. Prior to that Dick had been carrying Claes Oldenburg's plaster hamburger sculptures around in his jacket pockets. No one had ever done that before. In fact Oldenburg had created a little store shelf of hamburgers, hot dogs, and cakes.

AFTER CLEM GREENBERG'S DEATH, I had felt very alone. And then, as if recognizing the space, Dick appeared. It was a sort of absent-minded gift from timing, from the world. In my mind, in that secret rating system women maintain for their acquaintances, he'd always been a *yes*. But this was *wonderful* timing.

He was exquisite: perfect features and a shock of lustrous, straight black hair, which fell in one long brushstroke swipe across his forehead. One of Dick's habitual gestures—and, really, it took my breath away watching him—was to push aside his hair through the spread fingers of his left hand. Dick had started a number of careers along with Oldenburg's—there was Richard Serra's and Mark di Suvero's too, among others—and somehow this clung to him, the way a war hero's brave deeds come to precede him into a room. Dick was known to be hand in glove with the short, thin, and elegant Leo (Castelli) as well as two of his stars, Ellsworth (Kelly) and Jasper (Johns). And look at those names; I feel I've grown old enough now to draw some conclusions. And in the art world, I believe names can account for perhaps fifty percent of the impact in American art. Leo Castelli, Jasper Johns, Ellsworth Kelly, Jean-Michel Basquiat, Jackson Pollock, Brice Marden, Helen Frankenthaler—who *wouldn't* want to stick around for the rest of a story involving those exquisite names?

Dick had that essential knack so important in business of putting together the right rich person with just the right artwork, a canvas or sculpture selected by him. That is, artists loved Dick. He was able to make everyone happy with the contours and elegance of the deal—creators and buyers.

This meant he had to psych out the client, know what they would like. Then bring about that essential magical transaction: money for art.

DICK LEFT CINCINNATI at age nineteen. It is always strange—an inside joke—the somehow astray beginnings of people who become successful. Dick had traveled to the Hans Hofmann School in Provincetown, where he'd shed his clothes and worked as an artist's model. There was always that whiff of posed elegance about him. Dick attended college for one semester; his parents, both doctors, he said, "turned me off higher education." This was an element of the fifties that has somehow been shuffled aside. Dick had to do something else, something adventurous. He couldn't compete with them in a normal professional field. And he just caught on at the Hofmann School. Perhaps it had to do with his looks? He had the feminine perfection of the male faces in Matisse. After Provincetown, he came south to New York City and made his way. Physical beauty is a tremendous marker in the arts too—maybe even more here than elsewhere, though whose self-esteem isn't enhanced by the presence in their vicinity of beautiful bodies and faces? It can turn the beautiful heartless, knowing this is a wave they can ride to shore on. Turn them shallow.

Years in the art world had given Dick whole anthologies of great stories. One was about Jan Müller. A German painter who died at age thirty-six, Müller had rheumatic fever—possibly brought on by his splashing through cities and weather as a young boy, rushing from country to country to escape the Nazis. Shortly before Müller's death, Dick sold one of his paintings to the Museum of Modern Art for $1,500. He went to the bank, cashed the check, took payment in hundred-dollar bills. With another Castelli dealer—a man with the great name Ivan Karp—they sprinkled the cash across the floor of Müller's studio so that when the painter arrived home he found his waiting floorboards coated with money.

Dick was known to be a womanizer—that news reached me, as well. But too late, after I'd already become enthralled. The truth was I had always been interested in him. Not a huge roaring love. But one, as I said, that registered, "Yes."

IN THE MID-NINETIES when we started spending time together, he admitted to having been smitten back in the very beginning. It was the right thing to say, of course: Dick always knew the right thing to say. But I was also flattered to hear that over the years I'd left that low flame burning in such an estimable figure. And one I was attracted to as well.

And again, there was Dick's business side, the part other people didn't see. He reminded me he had come not just for the pleasure of viewing my work: he'd visited that old basement studio to select a painting for the novelist James Michener. He even knew the title, *Clear Music*. Had I asked, I am sure Dick would also have known the price. Dealers are like that. An anthology of the real, under-the-pasture tunnels and maintenance of the art world. All the deeds and contracts that keep the pastures grassy, the meadows unspoiled.

A few days after the sale, the phone had rung in our apartment. My husband had answered. "It's Dick Bellamy," he said, handing me the receiver. He had a wristless way of holding the receiver when a call wasn't for him—like a disappointing fish he was about to throw back. (All the spirit leaving his body.) I took the phone, and there was Bellamy on the other end, with what seemed like a party behind him.

"Can you meet for a drink right now?" he asked.

The only answer was no. My husband and children were beside me in our apartment, and I was too square for a date while married. This had already been a problem with my professor at Hunter. But I never forgot the call. I kept it in memory for revisiting and speculative enjoyment. He had wanted me.

A couple years later he started working on East Eighty-Second Street for someone called Noah Goldowsky. Sometimes, since we were still on East Eighty-Eighth, I'd stroll over just to see Dick, that beautiful aloof face the Hofmann students had painted in Cape Cod. Usually he'd be in the back office on the phone. That's what gallery people do: talk all day on the phone, often laughing with their heads tilted way back. As if to say, *Nothing is bothering me; all this, extracting dollars from the granite of culture, is as simple as turning the faucet, and my next sale is imminent.* I'd sometimes go to the Madison Pub—also on Eighty-Second—where Dick was a constant presence. Our desires run us through these small preliminary moves like chess pieces, at the start of what will be an involved and complicated game.

Once Dick asked me to store his large foam rubber Chamberlain couch in my loft. I said yes. And one day the amorphous piece of furniture arrived, then sat in the center of our main living space like a spongy, throbbing heart. What I returned to Dick four years later was a slimmed-down version; my sons had piteously plucked away much of the couch's yellowish foam rubber center, sitting inside its carved-out center watching TV, eating peanut butter crackers, and reading Marvel comics. They'd used little pieces of the Chamberlin as napkins.

IN THE 1980S he had a gallery overlooking the Hudson. A new neigh-borhood for the art world, a kind of SoHo satellite, on Chambers Street. Dick called it Oil and Steel. That's what you saw down there in lower Manhattan. He answered his own phone—it wasn't going entirely well, what the lack of a paid phone-answerer betrayed, but with his innate sense of grace he could make this sound natural, enviable. And even now, when I hear either noun, it somehow brings with it the sound of his voice, lifting the receiver: "Hello, Oil and Steel." This was another decade, and I needed a gallery. Although annoyed he wasn't showing my work, I let myself feel that—if you try to suppress a feeling like that, it finds a way to spread and poison everything—but still visited there a few times.

I had become a jogger, and Dick would phone to suggest I run downtown so he could give me what he called an après-jog massage. I never took him up on this. The bronze sculptures of vaginas by John de Andrea and Hannah Wilke he had scattered around the gallery's floor were a bit of a turnoff. I liked his Wallace Stevens come-ons better. That marvelous trained radio voice of his, in person, reading "The Poems of Our Climate" or "The Idea of Order at Key West."

I don't know when his physical troubles started. His body had brought him to the arts, and that same body now began to consider, and arrange the style and date of his exit. Another decade and his heart had started to fail. Dick needed a pacemaker. This is the phase he began referring to, breezily, as the Last Act. It began with his own heartbeat becoming unpredictable. His thirty-something girlfriend moved on to an age-appropriate partner. When I arrived for our second date, a rod of her skirts was still balanced across one wall of his bedroom. The clothes seemed to float there like the ghost of their relationship.

The first date was a SoHo opening for someone called Stephen Greene. Both of us had arrived separately. As I was leaving Dick asked if he could drive me home. For the first time in the decades I'd known him, the dealer looked breathless, in a hopeful way. Outside was his big white Pontiac. For reasons he never explained the sedan had a padlock on its front hood. When we reached—through the patterned overhead lights of the West Side highway and the squid night of the air above the river—my door on the Upper West Side he kissed me good night. Soft and sensuous. The kind of kiss that promised more without any special urgency. Really the best kind of first kiss.

Culture and being cultured seemed to embarrass him slightly. Maybe the old midwestern distrust of what's done on the coasts. He loved live orchestra music. To make them less snobby he called them *con-soyts*. We heard Mahler at Lincoln Center and again at Carnegie Hall. I reciprocated, asking him to dinner at my apartment. From Julia Child's fat book I spent hours whipping together her boeuf bourguignon.

That night we sat at the old 1812 school desk, which sometimes doubled in that apartment as a dining room table. Two dowels placed in holes on either side were supposed to keep it steady. My resourceful father had found and purchased it, then restored it. It was not meant to be eaten on, though, and so depending on which of us moved fork or knife, the tabletop tipped in that direction like a seesaw. Despite these unstable conditions only someone as smooth as Dick could have moved with such aplomb into my bedroom. At dawn he was lying there next to me.

THERE WERE OTHER COMPLICATIONS. As there always are, among the unmarried. Not just the recovery from the departed younger girlfriend. There was also an older woman—older than me—with whom he sometimes cohabited at Westbeth, the downtown artist's residence. From the way Dick explained this, it didn't sound entirely sexual. It sounded like an extended act of gratitude, penance for a good deed. She had nursed him back to health a few years earlier after his heart operation. Often, as he and I ate in his little Long Island City house, Marsha would call, and I'd listen to him economically and smoothly lie about what he was doing: another quiet evening at home, he'd say, or just settling in to read a new book. It always increases intimacy, that little shared thrill, to be on the other side of the lie.

Prior to our meetings, we'd consult by phone. He'd ask me to bring a book. Our dates consisted of us lying on his long, wood-frame futon, reading. A parody of the comfortable old couple we might have become, had we forsaken all others when we'd met. Sometimes he'd read poetry to me: John Ashbery, Robert Lowell. Solid poetry. One day Dick mentioned his first move into Proust. "I just bought *Swann's Way*. Roberta wrote in the *Times* that she's dipping into Proust too." That was Roberta Smith, then head art critic at the *Times*. Once he was firmly launched into *In Search of Lost Time* we talked over the fates of characters as if they were the art world figures both Dick and I had spent our whole lives among: Did I like Odette? And what did I think of Bergotte, the artist character who dies while looking at a dab of yellow sunlight painted on a wall by Vermeer? Did I, as a painter, find him believable? Did I, like him, despise the little clan of Madame Verdurin, and did they remind me, like they did Dick, of Roberta Smith and the many collectors who were guided by her dutiful, carefully phrased assessments about what was in and what was out? I remembered from reading the books that Proust had wanted his writing to be, he said, an optical instrument through which the reader would perceive her own life. And *The Search* became that for the life between me and Dick as well. Out of Proust, Dick created another link between us.

For dinner—near his Long Island City house—Manetta's Tavern with its fireplace roasting the backs of your knife, fork, and hands in winter. In Manhattan, Pig Heaven on the Upper East Side, a choice that confused me. Or Shun Lee, across from Lincoln Center, where, because there were two dining rooms, we once almost missed each other. We never visited a Japanese restaurant because Dick's mother was Chinese, and he gave me to understand that he—like other Chinese people from his era—hated the Japanese. Everyone brings to love a local history, with its local grudges. Sometimes we made love at two or three in the morning, fire trucks flashing quiet white lights across Dick's floor as they tucked themselves into the firehouse across his street.

No sirens, just lights. At the time I was fifty-five and Dick had turned sixty-eight, still full of elegant lazy life, even as his body seemed to pull in the other direction.

He talked about artists he'd been connected with. I imagined it as a partial tour of the twentieth-century collection at the Met, and a number slipped around angled corners of those galleries: Burgoyne Diller and Alfred Leslie, Myron Stout. A small red-and-white drawing by Diller hung over his bed. I kept waiting for Dick to pull out his own sheaf of poems, or the long novel that would be a gentle but ruthless exposé of the art world to which all of us had pledged ourselves. A ruthless, honest account by the sort of wise player who knew all the moves and the stories. But it never happened. I think he was one of the last true connoisseurs—an ardent appreciator of culture. And the connoisseurship was enough, did not have to be recorded. He liked that word, "ardent."

The other women fell away. And he no longer seemed to mourn the younger woman. One day her tinkling lines of skirts and blouses vanished from Dick's bedroom. Other pieces also vanished from the board. Dick's woman from Westbeth. It was a rounded-out story. We'd met, placed our casual marks on each other in our relative youths, and over the decades slowly but unerringly found the way back. Unhurriedly, we'd circled toward the center of the board, as time and happenstance lightened the squares of competing pieces.

A week before spring, there was an unseasonable, last-gasp snowstorm. I stayed with him all weekend, as I had begun to do. It is one of my favorite images of Dick, the simple one I would return to when there were no new ones to make. We woke to find his backyard covered. This innocent white snow. There was a sculpture out there; I didn't know who it was by, but suddenly it too was completely powdered and white. The way it would be if snow had fallen anywhere. In my grandparents' old bungalows, in China, or in Hans Hofmann's Provincetown.

He prepared the usual elaborate breakfast of bacon and eggs with meticulously diced green peppers, tomatoes, and onions. It looked like the makings of a chopped-up Oldenburg food sculpture. With toast and coffee.

After a couple hours I announced, "I'm going jogging."

Long Island City was more tricky than Manhattan. "Let me make you a map," Dick said, and he did that.

It was good following his directions, my feet stamping through crusts and untouched white, and once back in the warmth I asked for paper. Dick's advice here was clear. "Never draw on anything," he said, "but good paper." He was a dealer, after all: if it's good, if it's of any value, you might want to sell it someday. Anticipating my request Dick passed me some delicate rice paper, plus a small bottle of India ink and a brush. I did a version of his backyard in the snow. And left the sheet with him.

It was always horrible leaving. That part of being in love, which you think will diminish, stays with you. Around noon I thought it really was time to go. He accompanied me for the few blocks to the subway stairs. The two of us moving together through the snow-drift, low-building streets of Long Island City. The cold making ghosts of our breath, the way it did in childhood. As I went down the subway stairs toward the slushy, grimed platform, Dick stayed above in the square of daylight, watching me. I kept walking down those iron steps and finally when I looked up again he was no longer visible.

A few days after the storm Dick invited me to an opening for Lee Lozano—one of his artists in the sixties—at the Wadsworth Atheneum. We spoke the day before. He had been playing doubles tennis that morning and then lunched with his stepson and son. He sounded tired. Whatever these family occasions meant to him he kept to himself. When directly asked, he would say he'd done his duty, as if he had paid an emotional tax that was expected from him monthly. Duty was a big thing for him.

After two years of dating it was going to be our first public outing: an art world event at this Connecticut museum where we'd both know a lot of people. Lozano, terminally ill and living with her parents in

Dallas, was not attending. But her Wave pictures—ones he'd shown in the sixties—were being exhibited. Hartford is one of those eastern cities inconveniently serviced only by rail. We arranged to meet at Port Authority the next morning for the bus.

He still sounded winded from tennis, or whatever the son-and-stepson lunch had required. He asked what I was doing that evening.

Love is a flame that responds to deliberate tending. I said I had plans. I did not. But we'd both read in Proust that habit, perfect predictability, films over the luster of life. Proust's advice was that any relationship had to be carefully maintained and preserved by the shadow of infidelity. Really my only plan was to clean up, then buy Dick some Cheerios, because I knew he liked them. So when we returned from Connecticut my apartment would be clean and there would be something he liked to eat for the next morning's breakfast.

"Why don't you call me," he said cheerfully, "when you're finished with your whatever. And maybe you can take a cab out here and make me very happy?" I'd visited his little Archie Bunker house by cab so many times. I remembered being surprised the first time he took me there because it wasn't in any way cool, the way everything else connected with Dick always was. Just a defenseless white-box house with a white picket fence. Inside, there were rooster posters and little rooster sculptures, and the wood-framed futon.

The weather next morning was mild. I saw people outside in shirtsleeves—those tiny people you see through New York windows doing the brave work of assessing the weather for you—and thought my green Tahari suit would be perfect. I'd bought it for an art opening and since then it had become my default for romantic or important occasions. I dressed with great care.

It was a pleasure to meet a lover, even if at a bus station. Only when I arrived Dick wasn't at the ticket booth. This was unlike him.

What if he's not coming at all? I thought. *What if he's decided not to come?* I'd learned in love affairs that really anything was possible. Things that only visited characters in movies could trouble your real life. Once, when the Westbeth woman had fallen on the ice at the last minute, he'd canceled our date to see a George de la Tour show at the Met. I had that smarting sense of not being preferred, and the provocative idea that she'd timed the accident just to thwart me. I stood there a while longer, half expecting him to put his hands over my eyes, coming up from behind. But he simply and determinately refused with each passing minute to appear. I asked the gate number of the Hartford bus and jogged down to the lower level. It was almost nine. Our bus would soon leave.

He must be playing a trick on me. He'll be sitting on the bus smiling, I thought. But when I looked inside the bus what I saw was the famous scene of the Daumier third-class carriage, passengers neatly arranged in rows of seats, without Dick among them.

I found a phone booth and called. This is what I hoped would be the excuse: "Oh, I overslept. And I couldn't reach you." He didn't pick up the phone at all. I thought he might lift the receiver and say, "Hello, Oil and Steel." After what felt like a very long time, his son Colin, who lived in the house part-time, answered. He was an obdurate young man, prickly and faux-elegant—in the attempt to more closely resemble his father, who had achieved elegance without prickliness and with ease. To not grasp that was to misunderstand the attractions of his father.

"Hi Colin, it's Pat," I said. "Where's your father?"

"Dad died," he said.

Under the station lights, in this literally pedestrian setting, it was hard to make sense of what he'd said.

"He's dead," Colin repeated. And this is how stories end in real life. Not, as in Proust or Stevens, with decisions or reconsiderations or subtlety or charm. With brute, sudden, incontestable power. With interruption. With authority. Without elegance. Without art.

"How do you know?" I asked absurdly. Not waiting for an answer, I added, "I'll be right there."

The first thing I saw as the house rounded into view were two police cruisers with white eagles of snow across their hoods. And I knew then, knew in my stomach that it was true. I went in. Dick was still sitting up on that wood-framed futon, the Proust volume in his hands, a pencil nearby. I wondered if he'd been trying to write something before the spasms came.

Somehow, as time passed, seeing him dead there became easier than I could have imagined. Although it was unbearable to realize that one-half of everything we'd experienced together, one-half of all our jokes, all the time we'd spent sizing each other up from across our lives, all the shared judgments and experience, memories and reper-toire were sealed up and gone. And everything remained now with me, alone.

His glasses were on. And, touchingly, his teeth were out. I took the glasses. Looking through them was a way of seeing how he had seen the world. I am looking at them now.

"STUDIO"

HERE IS AN ATMOSPHERE. Your paintings are disarranged. Chairs now stare in many directions. Assistants are rubbing their heads and releasing great relieved gusts of air. You've just survived a studio visit.

Generally these require a few days of preparation. I've also pulled together a visit in forty minutes, but that takes fortitude and experience. The event itself is as wide with patience and tight with ritual as a late-night Christmas Mass.

You could face cancellations at the last minute, latenesses of one hour. Usually there's some explanation, like I was stuck on the West Side highway, but you still had to wait. And pay the assistants. Something about professional intimacy with art can breed in professionals a sort of compensatory ugliness. On the other hand, I've had a family of collectors—children, decorators, the mini-skirted art consultant, and an eighty-two-year-old matriarch who made the final decisions— arrive right at noon and leave ninety minutes later with $240,000 of stock.

At 10:35 a.m., I'm standing at my painting table. My assistant, Shala, waits beside my desk. Shala was born twenty-four years ago in Istanbul. And is at that moment of peak beauty. You can't imagine her features ever going that well together again.

She serves a sort of stewardess role: oversees greeting and departure. She'll welcome the visitor—the distracted critic, the resistant

dealer, the curator who will gossip about other painters then remi-
nisce about the curatorial program at Williams—and hand over the
packet stuffed with my reviews, profiles, and price list when the visit
is over.

SHALA ALSO HELPS with the waiting, speaks the anxiety I feel.

After about ten minutes, she announces, "This is very stressful."

Another responsibility is the phone. This is never answered with
"Hello." To convey the proper atmosphere of artistic endeavor and
wall-to-wall commerce, you simply say, "Studio."

The dealer Marlon Zwirsky is expected momentarily.

Zwirsky has a space on the Upper East Side. One of those tasteful
streets where the town houses stand together enjoying each other's
company. Setting up this visit took five emails. My triple-drafted
answers to the dealer's tossed-off questions. Zwirsky is scheduled to
arrive this February morning between 10:30 and 10:45.

Or did we finalize that? At 10:50, I start to wonder. I double-check
our email chain. A studio visit—because it's an assessment of quality—
is like being injected with a big hypodermic of doubt. Did I actually
receive a confirmation? Or was there some delusional misread on my
part?

No. There it is: with the fifteen-minute window because of a snowy
week. At eleven, when he still hasn't shown up, I dial Zwirsky's cell.

A mistake. When I say who it is, Zwirsky's voice gets weird. Like he
thinks my phoning is a complete faux pas. To her credit, Shala had
suggested I wait another ten minutes.

Zwirsky says, "I'm in the building."

The building: huge, and in the center of Chelsea. There are around
twenty other artists in the half-block former bookbinding factory. And
they're all competitors. (Only the freight elevator guys know who's
really doing well. And that's by following the number of paintings that
go in and out of studios.) It's a killer field. You could be very talented

and serious and still never make it to the top row. In fact, that's what's likely to happen.

We wait another ten minutes. Proust wrote that, in any situation, the victor is the person able to withstand pain one instant longer.

"I've got it," Shala announces. "He's in a building. It's just the wrong building."

There's a rap at the door. Shala jumps up to answer it. The two other assistants look over—I'll explain in a second—and at that moment we become a hungry and efficient family. All that matters is the skillful impression of smoothness and harmony we can create to show the paintings in the best possible light. We adjusted the window shades to let in the right amount of daylight between eleven o'clock and noon.

Shala comes back down the hall. And standing next to her is Marlon Zwirsky.

Tall and attractive, early sixties. Over her arm Shala holds Zwirsky's coat, which she hangs on a shiny hook I've screwed into the plaster. This is on a wall decorated with postcards of paintings I like, inspirational quotes, and photos of family members, some distant in time. Most painters' studios have a version of this wall. Under his coat Zwirsky is wearing jeans and a shirt with a fleece vest. I've got on jeans also, though my top is a black turtleneck sweater.

It's nice he's come alone. The big shot art types usually bring an entourage, including at least one very good-looking woman.

Zwirsky says hello, and I hear a tiny speech impediment. I have read online that he recently suffered a cerebral hemorrhage, then amazed his doctors by making a complete recovery. Still, there's a trace of something. It's in his words, like the ridge in the porcelain where a dish was mended.

"The drive took an hour," Zwirsky says. "The streets around here are really lousy."

This started as an apology but parks as an accusation. It's been snowing on and off all week.

"You're coming in from Millbrook?" I ask, to change the topic. Reading up on visitors before is a way, potentially, of getting an edge. You want to know as much as you can about the person before he shows up. Zwirsky's home, I learned, is in Millbrook, the sort of suburb real estate agents describe as an enclave. He also does something like photography in a big adjoining barn.

Still, visitors will say things that surprise you. This is a charged and information-rich encounter. Your career is on display for them: how far you've been able to go with what you think of as good. Your value on the market. But their whole life is on display too. How much taste do they have? How much money, influence, comfort, and satisfaction have they accumulated? (If they're not artists, they're accumulators. That's their career.) Once, two psychiatrists came. Prints only, they specified. No paintings—too expensive. The husband psychiatrist excused himself to the bathroom. The wife psychiatrist looked around wistfully. She sighed. "If I'd married a hedgie"—a hedge fund guy—"I could have bought anything I wanted."

"No," Zwirsky says. "During the week we've got a place on East Sixty-Fifth. Couldn't find a lot: I'm parked at a meter." He sizes us up, as if one of us might step forward to reveal an undisclosed world of parking. "I'm going to have to step out in forty-five minutes to go put money in the meter." He shakes his head.

For a studio visit, you set chairs facing your viewing wall so it resembles one row in a home theater. Next to that, a table with a painting list and some cold palm-size Poland Spring bottles. Zwirsky takes his chair aggressively, yanks it out of the careful alignment, and then flings his body onto it like a coat.

What am I thinking? In this situation, you're analyzing every statement at high speed for clues about taste, disposition, and outcome. (As well as income.) Like being in a play, you are focusing on the moment. You don't know whether the person is going to like the work or not. But you're trying to steer the conversation in ways that make you look good. First thing I think is: he plans on staying for at least forty-five minutes. Good.

I nod at my two other assistants, Gordon and Jackson. They will be moving and placing my big canvases. The hourly rate is forty dollars. I've hired many people to do this, and learned over the years that there is a type. Two types. The handsome, stringy, tattooed man in his late thirties who will turn out to know a great deal about penciling teams on certain classic runs of Marvel comics. This type was drawn to art by love of the painted square. And the shy art student in his early twenties. Unable to look you, or any creature, in the eye. This type dresses in chicly stained down coats, styles their hair in a hostile jumble. Jackson represents the younger type; Gordon the older version he might turn into. Both are members of the city's large and practically indispensable artistic underclass: the deliverers, helpers, handlers, hopefuls. But some of them, one way or another, work themselves up to doing well later. In that sense, *assistant* can be looked upon as an entry-level position.

Their job today will be to smoothly withdraw each work from the painting rack. Glide with it across the studio floor. Heft it smoothly to eye level, where the visitor can render a verdict. My paintings are heavy enough to need four strong arms. But when this goes right, you will not notice either man. Like dancers, they must have the ability to perform a demanding task in such a way as to leave no visible trace of the demand. Which is like a working definition of art too.

Jackson and Gordon bring the first canvas to the wall. Hoist it onto the viewing cans. You don't use wall nails because of the picture's weight. This lacks the playful studio touch of elegant improvisation one imagines when someone visited Picasso. We use two paint cans, upended. Paintings are placed on top of them and then leaned against the wall.

The first picture we set up this way is called *Proust's Sea*, a big, grayish seven-by-five-foot vertical. Zwirsky has apparently never heard or read this word. He is consulting the painting list with a skeptical expression. "Prowst?" he asks.

It won't go great this morning; you can sense it. I am not a bragging type of person. But I am totally brilliant at knowing how it's going to turn out. It reminds me of a line from a Victorian writer that every painter should know: *Any fool can paint a picture. It takes a genius to sell one.* (It was found in the writer's journal after death.)

I had a studio visit with the director from MoMA, where every element went off without a hitch. I was perfect; the paintings couldn't have looked better; he didn't try to speak with Gordon or Jackson; they didn't strike up conversations with him. And I could tell the whole time the museum wasn't ready to buy. There was even the nice, relaxed after-chat at the door. "Great making this discovery," the MoMA guy said. "Even if I *am* making it a little late." He didn't write a thank-you letter, always a good sign. That letter is death. It means a studio visit has devolved in their mind from business to something like a social call. And the whole time at the door, nodding and smiling, I kept thinking: *What would it cost them to buy? $125,000 to the MoMA is lunch.*

Gordon and Jackson have become faceless and smooth: disappearing one painting, manifesting the next. "I don't like these colors," Zwirsky says. And, "There's no *pop*." I always forget how Jackson, the shy student, blossoms in these situations. Becomes the dominant of the two men, issuing silent and expressing facial commands to Gordon, steering and stopping.

Marlon Zwirsky is what's called a fast viewer. A type that looks for one minute, then decides. I've noticed it is men who usually fall into this category. Women like to linger, discuss.

Half an hour has passed, and we're almost done. The rule of thumb is eight pictures an hour; you don't want to overdo. You want to pace it, best at the beginning, good in the middle, and then ending with a grand finale. This isn't going to take that long. We need to slow down. I look over at the pictures still to be shown, and suddenly they seem a sorry lot.

Zwirsky has slurped and swigged from his Poland Spring bottle. I take that as a cue to sip mine.

Jackson and Gordon are lifting a smaller square picture. Zwirsky made it clear in his emails that he prefers to see a variety of sizes. No response. So we put up *Reverse*. A tall vertical, with very firm reds, blues, and black. I'm aware this guy responds to bold color.

And he likes it! "Yeah . . . these colors," he says.

Fortunately I have executed three versions. Only the placement of the colors is different. Zwirsky glances at his watch. "Now I've gotta run downstairs and put money in the meter," he says.

While he's gone, Jackson, Gordon, Shala, and I pull out and unwrap the additional two versions of *Reverse*. Working silently and very fast.

These are casually out and waiting when he returns a few minutes later.

"How much is that?" Zwirsky points at the first in the series. There's still cool air coming off his body from outside, the way clothes are still chilly if you unzip your bag right after a flight.

"It would be eighty-five thousand at a gallery," I say. Actually, a low price for an established New York artist, where anything below a hundred thousand is considered shameful. "But as this is my studio there would be some flexibility."

"I can't pay that kind of money," he says. "No one's ever come into the gallery and asked for your work."

Jackson and Gordon glide out with the windup. A medium-sized black canvas, *Mithuna*.

This painting is named after a thirteenth-century sandstone piece from the Metropolitan's India wing. *Mithuna* sometimes gets translated as "loving couple," sometimes as the more clinical-sounding "sexual union." The Met sculpture is of a loving couple. I painted it in the '90s when I was in love. What I'd wanted was that calm that's sometimes in love: the reaching for what you know to be waiting. But the truth is that titles, for every painter I've ever known, come after. You paint the picture with no set idea. Then you give it a title almost randomly. And in the way of the mind's connections, these often fit, although you can't say why. Maybe because the person who made it and the person who titled it are the same person. They express you.

"I HATE BLACK PAINTINGS," Zwirsky says. He doesn't even bother to look. Instead he uses it as an opening to launch into his philosophy about the color black and his poor professional experiences with it.

"I have this black Norman Bluhm painting," he continues. "It's very big and takes two people to move, like yours. I've had it a long time. I can't sell the thing."

And with that, mercifully, the viewing ends. Gordon and Jackson lower their heads and step back from the viewing wall into temporary invisibility. That's part of their talent: knowing how to stand in a room in such a way as to attract not even a dust mite of attention. Shala knows she will soon be making sure Marlon Zwirsky leaves with my packet. I see her reach for it. The dealer lingers for another couple of minutes. I'm trying to connect with him. But it's like one of those dates where the man frustrates your intentions by throwing up a defensive fog of talk. Finally, all you can do is nod.

He mentions having bought twenty thousand paintings in his career. Zwirsky has just come out with a catalog of over seven hundred pictures.

"I usually buy a painting a day," he announces. Which, of course, I've read online. "There isn't a day that goes by when I don't buy some kind of major artwork."

In fact, that's the main reason he's sitting here in my studio. I gather my courage and ask, "What painting will you be buying today?"

He could say, "Yours." This would be so elegant.

Instead he says, "Somebody's coming by the gallery this afternoon to show me a couple of things. Maybe I'll buy one of his."

On his way to the door Zwirsky says, "We'll talk." This means nothing.

Shala closes the door and sort of laughs. There's the one-minute pause—to make sure your visitor has not left a coat, gloves, some

reflection of themselves. So they won't overhear. It's when the minute has passed that you know you've survived a studio visit. Everyone
can speak again. Resume their normal lives. The two painting-movers
crack their backs and let out audible breaths. I sort of laugh.

"Wow. That guy was an asshole," Shala says.

"Com*plete* and *to*tal asshole," Gordon specifies, and Jackson, head
down, grins. And there is the end picture, the final image the visitor
never gets to see, ninth in the series. The bottles, the canvases out,
the chairs, the assistants restored to themselves, to their personalities
and lives. They want to know what I thought. I shake my head and say,
"Disaster." They laugh.

Then we look up. Footsteps are coming back down the hall. We *have*
been overheard. But it's Donovan, the upright, uber-competent man
who oversees the building. And when he steps in, sees the four of us, I
am struck with a sudden happiness. And so what he views is the tenth
picture. The one that I didn't know we made. Of me, inhabiting this
studio. A fierce happiness. My paintings are out. With assistants. I did
the work. And I've managed to hold on to it, protect it this long.

FIFTH AVENUE

IT WAS ONE OF THOSE buildings on Fifth Avenue where an impeccably polished wood-paneled elevator opens into a single apartment. I was visiting the eighth floor, so when the elevator stopped, since the door was open I walked right in. It was the apartment of someone I'd dated in college, Benjy Serchuk.

Immediately it felt claustrophobic in a familiar way—like the homes of parents I'd visited in exclusive Jewish enclaves like Great Neck and Scarsdale. Over the apartment's wall of windows facing the street hung long white satin curtains topped with an elaborate valence treatment. Behind which was a view of Central Park, now hidden.

I couldn't imagine why anyone would block it. Maybe Benjy and his wife, Gloria, were modest? Or, perhaps it was something practical; someone in their family had skin cancer, for which sunlight was verboten? There were other possibilities too—maybe closed white satin curtains are part of a religious ceremony I know nothing about? Regarding a view, Gertrude Stein wrote, "I like a view but I like to sit with my back to it."

Some of the apartment's other furnishings were more predictable—a dark green velvet couch and matching chairs, with a heavy wood coffee table in between. An intricate mahogany sideboard above which hung a Milton Avery landscape, all green too. I thought I might see a Tom Wesselmann, one of his tacky pop American nudes. (One day sometime before, I'd bumped into Gloria rushing out of Christie's,

where she mentioned having just placed a pre-auction bid on a Wesselmann.) But there wasn't one up.

THE APARTMENT'S SMELL—somewhere between the odor from mat-
zoh ball soup left standing and day-old Jell-O—was also familiar. It
brought to mind those same Westchester and Long Island locations
from my past.

Gloria wasn't there. Years before she'd gotten an advanced degree
in education, an EdD, which had never quite moved her up to PhD
status. Not that it mattered, since she didn't work in education anyway.
Everywhere she was listed as a "philanthropist." Gloria donated huge
amounts of money to Benjy's Ivy League alma mater. It meant both
their children would probably be granted admission because their
parents funded so many university programs. "Glor," as she was called
among intimates, had been high up in the Clinton machine during
Hillary's two failed attempts at the presidency. In fact, she was one
of the five biggest donors to their campaign chest. When the Clintons
moved one town over from the Serchuks' home in Westchester, Gloria
carried a home-cooked meal to them for their first dinner.

WHEN I ARRIVED, Benjy Serchuk, just under six feet tall, was loung-
ing on the couch. Although he was pushing eighty, the new sixty in
Manhattan, he hadn't put on any weight since college. He was wearing black felt pants and a blue T-shirt. Below his huge forehead sat a
bulbous nose. His hair, what little was left of it, hung down as if he'd
formerly been in the recording industry. His feet were bare. Something I'd noticed, particularly among Jewish men, was that they liked
walking around barefoot. It showed how far away they'd moved from
one of the Talmud's dictates: "A person should sell the roof beams of
his house to buy shoes for his feet."

BENJY SAW ME and signaled that I sit down on one of the dark green
chairs. A flowered pitcher and two water glasses graced the coffee

table. As did decorated dessert plates, each holding a tiny fork as in Soutine's *Still Life with Herrings*. I hoped they meant that at some point tea and biscuits would be served.

As we started talking you could hear voices speaking Spanish in another room. And then, straight out of a forties Hollywood movie, a woman with a rose in her hair came in to give Benjy a handwritten message. Nothing was said.

"Do you ever look out the window?" I asked, nodding at the curtained wall.

"Nah," he said, "there's really not much to see. Just the traffic coming down Fifth and then, you know, Central Park. If I want to take a walk I can always drive up to our place in Mt. Kisco—it's only an hour away."

"Wow, I'd look out the window all the time if I lived here. *And*, walk in the park," I said.

Serchuk turned ever so slightly toward me and said, "What I'm into now is rowing." I had to suppress the words *Row, row, row your boat*, which immediately came to mind. He spoke with a kind of dazed slowness, as if full enunciation would take too much out of him.

"Yeah, a couple of years ago I rowed down the Charles River, the whole eighty miles of it," he said phlegmatically.

"That must have been exhausting," I answered.

"Really, it wasn't that bad. Now I own three row clubs. I'm driving to one right after you leave. Then next week I'll be in Fort Lauderdale rowing at another of my clubs."

WHEN WE WERE IN OUR FORTIES, Serchuk and I had become reacquainted. It happened one day when we were both jogging around the reservoir, he in one direction, I in the other. Sometimes I'd see Dustin Hoffman on the same trail. At the time I was training for the New York Marathon. Not Benjy. He was training for the much more difficult, and newer, triathlon. It involved swimming, biking, *and* running. I'd heard he'd had an indoor swimming pool installed at his Mt. Kisco home so he could practice laps.

Without my asking, Benjy felt called upon to fill me in on his and Gloria's lifestyle. "We spend fall, winter, and spring right here, and go for weekends to Westchester."

"What do you do in the summer?" I asked right on cue.

"Oh, we're at the Vineyard then, with Bill and Hillary."

"That must be great," I said. As with many rich men, he asked me *nothing*. My unstated role in the conversation was simply to keep the questions coming, like a coach pitching to players during batting practice.

"Of course, when the kids were growing up we lived *exclusively* in Mt. Kisco because of the school." (Implying that the Karafin School was better than either Trinity or Dalton in Manhattan—that is, *if* they could have gotten in.)

In the background I could still hear female voices speaking Spanish, and glasses and silverware clinking together like a jazz club on Friday night.

Once location was covered, Benjy moved on to gossip—who had recently remarried or divorced, who had passed away. Jerry Kalvin, someone we both knew from college, had married another architecture student straight out of school. Then after twenty-five years he decided to split. Right then his wife developed a rare form of cancer that made it impossible for him to leave. But the moment *after* she died, Kalvin married his best friend's *daughter*.

"Can you imagine," Benjy said. "He's having sex with his friend's daughter, who is the same age as one of *his* daughters and a friend of hers." Actually I thought Benjy could imagine it very well.

Interesting. Now marrying your best friend's wife is déclassé—the newest thing is to marry your best friend's daughter (or son).

After gossip we moved on to reminiscence: here it seemed I was to play a bigger role. Ben brought up driving to my parents' house all those years ago. To borrow Proust's metaphor, because of our advanced ages he and I were standing on long stilts that represented the time we had lived. They carried us all the way back to Christmas break, 1961.

"Your mother was a force," Benjy said, "and your father, he was totally enigmatic. I really liked their house too, all those antiques."

"Thanks," I said. "Remember when we first met, a year before that? I was a freshman and I think you were just starting senior year." The sound of silverware still clanking in the background. "You pulled up in your blue convertible—top down—next to where I was standing on Seneca Street and asked who I was."

"Pat Sutton," I said.

Then you asked where I was from and I answered, "Brooklyn." You laughed. People used to laugh back then if you said you were from Brooklyn.

"Can you meet me at Zinck's tomorrow night at seven?" you asked. "We'll have dinner."

Although I had no clue where Zinck's was, I managed to find it the next night, my pageboy still intact. Then I had the nerve to order steak. You must have told everyone, because around campus I suddenly became known as "the steak girl."

Benjy laughed, and then went on. "I kind of remember the steak," he said. "But you know, Pat, we only went out a couple of times."

"Really, that's what you think? I remember more like every Friday night my freshman year. Your frat, Pi Sigma, would have a party, and when we arrived Steve Mailman would be standing on the porch like a figurehead on the prow of a ship."

"Yeah, I remember that," Benjy said. "Mailman was sort of the frat's maître d'."

"There'd be a live band playing, something from Elvis—maybe 'Heartbreak Hotel,'" I continued. "Well since my baby left me / I found a new place to dwell / It's down at the end of Lonely Street at Heartbreak Hotel / You get me so lonely baby, you get me so lonely I could die.

"You and I would start dancing the Lindy, you keeping the beat with your left hand as you swung me out, and back, with your right." (I could still picture this, Benjy biting his lower lip with his upper teeth, which

I found very sexy.) "After a few slow and fast numbers we'd be sweating like crazy. And that's when the inevitable argument would occur."

"I remember dancing," Benjy said. "And I remember arguing. But I have no idea what we argued about." And then he leaned over and whispered, "You know, Pat, you and I were never intimate."

That made me laugh out loud, as if I needed Benjy to tell me who I'd slept with. "Of course I know that," I said.

Right after that a different maid walked in with a tray that had a jug of water on it and poured some into the two glasses. There was no mention of tea.

We got up. Adjacent to the living room were French doors that led into a dining room. At the center sat a large round table with a white tablecloth and twelve elaborate place settings. Three Latina ladies, including the one with the rose in her hair, were sitting and talking.

"Gloria's having a dinner party tonight," Benjy explained. "They've just been setting the table. I'm driving up to Mt. Kisco."

On one wall I could see a Frankenthaler print, and on the other a Ray Johnson collage. He was called "a mail artist" because a lot of his "art" involved sending letters back and forth. Hanging there was one of his postcards, with the recipient's address and some cartoons. "How moving," I said.

"Yeah, we really enjoy it," Benjy answered, "it kind of grows on you."

AS WE WALKED back into the living room and toward the open door beyond which was the vestibule, I said, "Good seeing you."

"Good to see you too," Benjy said.

Then I pressed the elevator button, and once it came, the L button for lobby. When I stepped out onto Fifth Avenue the air was fresh.

EDGES

IN GRAD SCHOOL I learned that art school can be highly territorial. Most everyone stakes out a location in the studio on the first day of class, and it's theirs for the remainder of the year. Fights erupt if somebody tries to take another person's spot. By chance Sharon Fliss wound up next to me that first day. We had all our painting gear with us and dropped the stuff down on neighboring tables.

I was twenty-four at the time. By then I'd had two children. Sharon was my age and had one child. Precociously, she'd already been divorced. Hard to believe our lives, apart from making art, were the norm for many twenty-four-year-old women back then. Divorce, too, was soon to be the norm.

In addition to our children and our age, we both lived near Hunter on the Upper East Side. A few weeks later she confided that her marriage to Fliss had been brief, and that she'd returned home when it ended. She told me her mother was deaf, and that she took care of the baby when Sharon was in class.

Not that I imagined my marriage would come apart then, but if it had I couldn't simply have returned home like Sharon. By then, my mother was off the rails. She'd always been difficult—overbearing, self-involved, and lacking impulse control. But she'd been graced as well with warmth, wit, intelligence, and, in her early days, great beauty. Then, in her forties, she started taking a prescription drug called

Darvon. This was when some doctors had begun prescribing mood-altering drugs for women, to cure the mildest and most random complaints. She'd have outbursts of temper between doses, which would ramp up her criticisms of me. I had no clue where this was coming from.

I went to college, got married, and had children. Once out of school, I decided to see a therapist. My father knew about it and, in a weak moment, told my mother *everything,* including the therapist's name. My mother then, in her attempt to control the therapy, phoned my therapist many times a day. Finally, the doctor suggested I seek treatment elsewhere.

IN THE '60S we fine arts grad students would sit around after class discussing Abstract Expressionism. One conversation I remember centered on our favorites—Pollock, Rothko, Newman—and how they'd gotten their effects. What sticks in my mind was the fascination Sharon and I seemed to share regarding Rothko's technique, specifically how he handled the edges where colors come together—that seductive moment in abstraction where two colors touch.

Sharon was talented. She was painting right next to me, so I could see everything she did. For instance, she was using raw canvas rolled out and stapled to her painting table and was applying the paint with kitchen sponges.

I thought she had integrated some of the stuff that made Rothko so exceptional. And wanted to copy her technique, but needless to say, I couldn't right then. So I stored the idea for some other time and continued working with hardware store house painter's brushes. But those had already been mined. Only much later did everyone learn, in a book by one of Rothko's assistants, that he'd gotten his blur from nothing more than a conventional fan brush. Not surprising, really, since Rothko saw himself firmly entrenched in a tradition going back to the Renaissance.

Sharon and I were friendly outside of class. She confided in me about the *earthshaking* affair she had with another student—a dark, Sicilian roué named Andrés Colazo. As graduation approached, I decided to apply for the Fulbright scholarship. I learned six months later that the US committee had approved my application, but the Spanish government—I'd applied to go to Malaga—didn't grant its approval because I would be bringing my husband and children. It would have been no problem, of course, if I'd been a man bringing *his* wife and children. At least I got some good news from the Fulbright guy who told me I hadn't gotten the scholarship: he offered me a studio.

The empty apartment was right around the corner from where we lived on East Eighty-Eighth. The first thing I did was paint the walls white. Then I went to the neighborhood drug store and bought out every sponge they had. On raw canvas in lightest pencil I plotted logarithmic curves in sequence from small to large. Then came the paint. I laid the canvas out, wet it down, and began sponging the thinned acrylic paint up and down the curves. Soon my edges were blurry— colors alluringly bleeding into one another.

BACK IN COLLEGE, when I was looking for books in the library stacks, I would often run into a guy named Stephen Muller. He wore steel-rim glasses long before they were popular. Ditto his dark turtleneck sweaters. Stephen had a funny way of talking, as if his words had to cross a rocky shoreline before entering the world of speech. Despite that, once the senior guys I'd been dating were gone, I flirted with him a few times.

Nothing came of it. But later it appeared we were still in a mysterious orbit. So one day, in Manhattan, he told me there was going to be a party. I couldn't go because there was no babysitter available. But then to my surprise, almost as if I were hearing my grandmother, Nana, and my great aunts' voices in the next room, the urge to matchmake came over me and I mentioned the party to Sharon. Maybe she'd meet someone there? She took the address, but said probably she'd pass because of cold sores on her face. Yet the next day, she reported that she and Stephen had hit it off.

NOT TOO LONG AFTER MY arrival at the first studio, I started getting noticed as a painter. Art dealers had heard about me and were interested in my work. I got many unsolicited studio visits and soon had a big-name gallery. And then the paintings started selling, selling as fast as I could paint them.

Around the same time, Sharon set up a studio. As I recall, it was an empty room she rented in a commercial loft. Here, too, she seemed adventurous. Downtown lofts, converted small-scale manufacturing spaces from the nineteenth century, were pretty much unknown then, although five years later everyone would have one. However, when Sharon invited me over, the pictures she pulled out were unresolved, timid. Though I didn't say anything, I was shocked by this regression from her grad school work. At times since, I've felt guilty about not offering her the advice that seemed so obviously right that day. But probably I didn't want to risk my lead by helping her.

A few years later I was making serious money and having my first exhibition at Emmerich Gallery. I think Stephen and Sharon, married by then, showed up for the opening. The pictures sold out within a week, cementing my momentary status as the New York art world's It Girl. There was even a column about me in *Vogue*.

Then, "the dog barked and the caravan passed"—Proust's description from *Swann's Way* of fashion's brisk movement. I lost track of the Mullers, though at one point I heard Sharon had quit painting and gone to law school.

Chance seemed intent on bringing Sharon and me back together. My younger son was in high school and one day I overheard him on the phone mention Zack Fliss. Now our sons were in the same school. Then in the late nineties Stephen and Sharon emerged as art collectors, directors of the Sharon and Stephen Muller Art Fund. I saw them more than once in Chelsea—Sharon always walking behind him, as if they thought New York were Calcutta. One time, we stopped to talk.

Stephen had given up his ascetic look. Instead, he was always ready with a joke or pun in case the conversation flagged. Maybe this was how he'd imagined himself back when his speech had been labored. He bragged to me about being part of the machinery of the New York art world, the vital part as far as an artist is concerned: collector. My studio was now in Chelsea, just blocks from where we were talking, and I suggested they stop by sometime.

A month later Sharon phoned. The ensuing studio visit involved extensive preliminaries. Sharon never gave me her email address. Plans were to be made by phone, and only when she called me. Finally, the visit was settled. Stephen wouldn't be attending. Which should have told me the visit would be a waste of time. (Without the husband nothing sells.) Preparations are elaborate, including training the hourly assistants.

Sharon and I were now in our late fifties, keeping age at bay through diet, exercise, and prayer. She arrived at the studio on the appointed day wearing slacks, a wide belt, a loose sweater. I went with my typical painter's minimalism—jeans and a black turtleneck. Soon, my two young assistants were pulling out one picture after another, placing each on an empty, immaculately painted white wall. Sharon sat motionless, hands folded in her lap.

Once the viewing was over she opened up. Was even expansive, as she told me about her and Stephen. About their lives and their art fund. She explained what the fund acquired—mostly minimalist pieces done by people they hung out with, the price for their admission. I suggested she and Stephen stop by my Chelsea gallery, but Sharon said they only visited galleries on the Lower East Side.

THEN CAME THE EARLY 2000S. It was a bleak time for me, and everyone else in Manhattan. In Chelsea, for weeks after 9/11, we could still smell the ash of burning flesh from the World Trade Center.

My sales were down. And that continued until after the Lehman Brothers debacle. I made more from shipping damages to my paintings than I did from new collectors. My meticulous and heavily layered canvases from that period proved surprisingly fragile, and more than a few were destroyed by notoriously careless art movers who transported them to living room walls "on approval," where they were tested to see if they really fit into the collector's home. So, for a time, insurance proved my best collector.

These pictures represented my distillation of aesthetic experience. But by then the art world at large had little interest in being moved by art. That had been substituted by the boring area of personality. Collectors were interested in buying access into an artist's persona, their story, struggles, and disadvantages. Or political art, especially by people of color. To mirror identity politics. Objective quality was out.

In fact, art that disowned aesthetic experience entirely—a shark in formaldehyde or a banana duct-taped to a wall—was sought after. Even more absurd, differentiating between good and bad made people uncomfortable. Including, surprisingly, the director of the Metropolitan Museum. (He refused to allow those terms to be spoken at staff meetings.) As if any kind of differentiation was a slight against democracy. Shock art, and celebrity art—who the artist is, who she hangs out with, what drugs she takes or has taken, has she been raped—these were the interests of the moment. Plus, art by every minority group except Jewish.

A JOB TEACHING figure drawing at the Manhattan Institute came up. The class ran month by month, with no prerequisites. Anyone could sign up. One day, I came into class, and standing across the studio was someone who looked disarmingly like Sharon, back when we'd been at Hunter. I started making the rounds, talking with each student about their drawings. When I got to the new student, she said, "Yes, I'm Sharon." For a drawing class she was strangely accessorized—big diamond earrings, several rings on her fingers, one of which was another diamond, a Cartier watch. Her buffed and clear-coated nails spoke eloquently: I am rich, I am sturdy, I am well cared for.

Only then did I look into her face, "hollow of cheek as if she drank the wind." We were, by then, both in our early seventies, but a professional had gathered the skin of her face and artfully pulled it back.

She made it to one out of every three classes and never stayed to the end. Sometimes her cell phone rang and she'd rush out to meet Stephen, apparently still in a Lower East Side gallery. If art class was her private therapy, then collecting was couples therapy, and it took precedence.

Otherwise she'd leave class because she was drained: "I have to go home and rest now." It was an invidious comparison; as a salaried employee I was required to stay to the end.

Sharon arrived tanned and healthy in what turned out to be her penultimate class. She described Art Basel in Miami as an incongruous pairing of Old World solemnity—Art Basel in Basel and the gaudy New World—Art Basel Miami Beach. What had been proven was that rich people liked to be seen in public writing huge checks. After class I looked the Mullers up on Google, and there they were, their attendance noted among other collecting luminaries: for instance, the Rockefellers, Rothschilds, and Mortimers. And then a few artists' names thrown in for authenticity: Cindy Sherman, Lisa Yuskavage, and Jack Pierson.

Sharon was early for what proved to be her last class. With a new alacrity, she finally finished a good drawing of the seated male model. I told her so. She was clearly pleased, which seemed almost to speed her on her way. "I'm going to quit while I'm ahead," she said as she packed up her supplies. I never got to tell her I'd stolen her painting style forty years before.

WHO THEY WERE

ISAAC WITKIN came from South Africa, full of promise. On the basis of some of his London sculptures and being Henry Moore's assistant, he was given a Bennington College teaching spot and a faculty house on campus. Isaac was twenty-six.

He had two little daughters with Thelma. People were paying a lot of attention to him then. Isaac had trained in London before coming over, and in the beginning, I guess, thought he would eventually be heading back. A big beautiful man, strong-handed, with a black beard.

CLEM GREENBERG didn't like Isaac's work. And Isaac didn't listen to him. Clem would go up to Bennington to see the "Bennington Sculptors." They'd all come out in the snow for a few days of critique. Wool scarves, boots. And Clem would make suggestions—do this, do that. "Go higher," or "build out." Isaac didn't like it, didn't listen to him. He didn't care what Clem advised. He thought, "Fuck that." Isaac was from a rich family. His mother had been a concert pianist and was a grande dame in Johannesburg. The worst was when Greenberg compared Isaac to the Abstract Expressionist Adolph Gottlieb, whose work everyone knew Clem didn't like.

So that was that.

PEOPLE WHO CAME to SoHo were painters, sculptors, and the Mafia. Pretty much everybody I knew lived nearby, so it was like this cast-iron

front that had a clearing every few blocks where a friend lived. Dan
Christensen was up the long streets over on Waverly, in a loft rented
to him by New York University; Larry Poons was two blocks away on
Canal Street; around the corner on Greene Street was Peter Reginato;
and prior to his misfortunes Ken Greenleaf was on Crosby. It made
the street names exciting, each one secretly inhabited. That feeling of
youngness is part of this. The city seemed not stone and edges but a
single overarching friend made of component welcoming parts.

Most of us had mob neighbors. The building across our street was
mob. Somehow roughed-up-looking, with this slew of garbage trucks
out front that thrashed around mostly in the early morning hours.
One day I walked over to see about the noise. I climbed up the outside
steps gummy with bird shit, then climbed the dark creaking staircase
covered with rat shit and entered a dirty office with one employee.

"We're just across the street," I said, pointing a thumb over my
shoulder. "I wonder, could you keep the trucks quiet early? They're
waking everybody up."

The guy tilted for one second and I felt that chill glimmer of threats
being considered. He had wide shoulders. His hair was thick and wavy
black. "What time are you talkin'?"

"Around seven thirty?"

"*Sure,*" he said. Only it came out as two syllables. *Shoo-ah.* And that's
exactly what he did. The building is now a sleek white and friendly
structure called the Drawing Center. The two main galleries when I
started—André Emmerich and Leo Castelli—were like warring nations,
in a state of perpetual hostilities. You were with one or the other. No
artist was nonaligned, and every artist I knew wanted to be with either
of those dealers. They showed different work and stood for different
things: Castelli, pop art, and Emmerich, color field painting.

There was a premium then on being an artist. Castelli wouldn't
have taken us anyway. Our art had too much feeling. When I met Leo
Castelli—with his sensitive jaw and big egg eyes—he didn't mention
my paintings. He had an elegant velvet aura. He held my hand in his

soft palms. Told me I was beautiful. André was bigger, more square-jawed: a man in a double-breasted jacket on the deck of a yacht. Two different approaches to the kind of power they had. André wanted you to know he had power: Castelli's thing was, you could notice his calm and figure it out.

He handled a lot of pop artists—James Rosenquist, Roy Lichtenstein, Jasper Johns, and others. We thought pop was shit. Too easy to like. You never want to find yourself on a side fighting against the thing that's easy to like. It's like trying to argue people's taste buds out of sugar. Years later, Dick Bellamy and I were in bed at his Chambers Street loft when, with that slow, truthful, calm voice of his, he said, "Lipsky, you chose the wrong group." It didn't feel like that then.

These were the years when you opened the Friday art section and what you saw was about your friends. Which means it was also about you. And sometimes, of course it was about you. When I got divorced, it was in the paper. When, for a time, I returned to my pre-married name, that got reported too. The attention was just another element you lived in. You were interesting to other people. And the ads for the galleries were about you or your friends. A name that has a particular meaning for strangers—a certain glamour, a certain slant on style. It made the world of success feel like a second home that someone had tossed you the keys to. It can be the giddiest feeling. Like having your veins surging with more than the standard allotment of blood.

CLEM MADE ISAAC WITKIN ANGRY. Isaac would say, in that powerful deep-voiced accent, "I mean, but seriously, where does the man come off? He isn't an artist." I loved him a little bit. For a man of his size and character he had very soft, gentle tastes. His brother sang opera in London. On the other hand, Isaac loved boxing, the smash and intimacy, two men demolishing each other. He had boxing magazines everywhere. He loved wrestling too. I told him a thing I remembered from a Proust book: "Those who produce works of genius are not those who live in the most delicate milieu, who have the most brilliant conversation, the most learned culture, but those who have had the power . . . to make their personality similar to a mirror."

THE BOXERS, Stanley and Joyce, were New Yorkers with heavy accents and the hard manners of another era—that rowdier time that always seems to have ended about a decade and a half before whenever now is. My children loved Stanley because he was good with kids, could do a squint like Popeye's, and since he and Joyce had no children there was a lot of surplus affection to go around. When one of the kids accidentally put his foot through their skylight they were incredibly nice.

Every morning Stanley walked into his studio and thought, "I am going to be great." Stanley was so thin. The other thing Stanley told himself was "Maybe I am the best of my generation." And I think Joyce believed that about him. A lot of us did, painters in our thirties. At the time you don't really know how it's going to pan out. He gave the paintings optimistically poetic titles like *Unctionpalesinbalmofsnow*. His Wikipedia entry now averages four page views per day.

THE DIFFERENCE, for us artists, was that Leo Castelli came from Trieste money. He thought like a rich person—the solid confidence of knowing there would always be more. And André, who had grown up without luxury in Amsterdam, had the poor person's anxiety. When his family fled the Nazis and got to New York in 1939, they moved to Queens. For someone like André, that must have been hard. Plus, there was no money for college and he had to accept a scholarship to Oberlin, where he also waited tables. So one can understand his caution about money even when things got better and he had his own very successful art gallery. That nagging suspicion that, at any given moment, there could once again be less.

Castelli paid his artists a stipend: sell or fail, fair weather or drizzle, they'd be taken care of, kept warm and dry. It gave them freedom to try things. But those of us who depended on André were just out there, wired on our own success and nerves.

IN THE SEVENTIES Isaac showed at Marlborough. Big space, perfect for his sculpture. And then they kicked him out. The guy who had been his contact, Jacque Monyez, died suddenly while playing tennis. Who could have predicted it? Many of these arrangements hang by a single thread. A strong wind like that and they're gone.

Isaac knew how to manipulate things so the gallery would pay his making costs—i.e., what it costs to have the piece fabricated from the initial clay maquette into steel or bronze. Marlborough laid that money out up front so his big steel or bronze sculptures could be fabricated and then exhibited. Once Monyez was gone the owner, Pierre Levai, didn't keep up the arrangement. Isaac was out.

Then he went to Hirschl & Adler. That wasn't going to be as good. Smaller space, and not on Fifty-Seventh Street. I remember one Saturday sitting at an outdoor tea place on Madison Avenue, near Seventieth. (Hirschl & Adler was then on Seventy-Ninth.) Isaac had left the gallery and was walking down Madison. He spotted me at the café and crossed over. Smiled and sat down. We drank tea. (Sad to think about now because it can never happen again.) Someone else, no doubt, will be walking on Seventy-Ninth and turn down Madison, but he wouldn't be Isaac. And I wouldn't be sitting at a café nearby sipping tea.

YOU PRINTED YOUR OWN CURRENCY. People were always happy to see us. You could trade paintings for a new kitchen. For dentistry. For the lobster and steak at Max's, and everybody's drinks.

Dan Christensen traded our company for two years beside the Southampton beach. A rich woman believed four painters and three sculptors installed in her guest cottages would be to her social advantage. At night the dunes became cool, slippery, and ominous. And the ocean turned out to have many more moods than the few sparkling impressions you gathered during a summer's day. Resentful, powerful, gracious, indifferent, repetitive, obliterative, seething. You got to know them as you would the facial expressions of a lover.

You'd step off the midnight train into this quiet town with the sweet smell of lawns and money. Another private joke: strolling these avenues of titanic fortune, with our raucous dungaree energy. The same Black cabdriver, our friend, always dropped us on Dune Road. His trunk creaked when you yanked out your bags. He always said, "The Truth shall set you free." And then puttered off into the night, leaving you with the folding crack of the waves, the somehow intimate ocean smell that fed your nostrils, the unbelievably lush nighttime blue overhead, the crickets purring so loud they sounded like sleigh bells. And once our driver had pulled away, Dan said, "Yes. But it's reviews and sales that get you beachfront."

MICHAEL STEINER came from New York. A sculptor with a big bald bullish head and confidence that can become grabby. This quality was like a dog standing guard above the dish; it wanted to make you think it would gobble up all the good fortune in the world. You'd tell a positive story, then Steiner would brag you away from the table with an even bigger one.

Isaac thought Steiner was a fake. "There are passages of sheer brilliance in Michael's work," he said. "And then he ruins them with a single stroke." But everybody else—Larry, Dan, Poons, Saito—was impressed by Michael. I think they were intrigued by his confidence. A vivid, aggressive enjoyment of life: it can take you pretty far.

It can be especially attractive to collectors. When you're spending tens or hundreds of thousands of dollars on an artwork, lack of confidence may not be the prime quality you're after. Insecurity is one of the great writing themes. It's comparatively absent from the visual arts.

Years later, Steiner had a show in Newburgh, New York. This was very far from Emmerich and Castelli. But it's what an artist does.

Given the opportunity, you show. The reviewer was Australian, thirty-six years old—hardly born when Steiner had been the loud voice you could hear from so many tables away. He was the future that arrives to judge with innocent eyes. "Abstract sculpture slipped into the waste-basket of art history," went his piece in the *Times*, "because there were not enough good artists doing it."

I had an image when I read this of Michael and his damp bald head. All of it—the growling at others, the purring over himself—had been a hedge against this future, a hedge that had failed.

DAN CAME FROM the Kansas City Art Institute. He was so watchful. I guess when you've traveled to the more famous city, resolved on success, it's the way you have to be. You accept the greater density of things worth paying attention to. He was sharp, even about me. That night at Max's I was in a sulk, and people kept coming up to me: "You're showing with André. You have two kids. Things are going great." And Dan became angry. "What's great about it? She just got divorced. The ex-husband is giving her a terrible time—what's great about that?"

We threw parties together, three or four very long blowouts a year. Looking at me one night Dan said: "You're the queen of SoHo." All the parties celebrated the same basic fact—us being artists, friends, successes together. Dan was always arranging things. He'd wake every-body at dawn to go bluefishing, baiting the hooks by flashlight, all our fishing poles dug into the sand, casting pale shadows as the sun came up.

It was when he was drunk that Dan relaxed. Then his eyes settled, his arms went rubbery. Even his mustache looked drunk. My sons loved him. He had the kind of drunk personality children appreciate: where the barriers between adult and kid drop. They had endless pine-cone fights, Dan winging the green spiny cones so hard it hurt. For a boy, this amounted to respect. Later, when we weren't at the same gallery anymore and Dan became so distant to me, what seemed egre-gious was how he could be so chilly to the kids he had let so excessively love him. It seemed somehow *untruthful*. It was me who was subject to the risk of this being only a temporary friendship—that it was always success that had been celebrated more than the alliance—and how, especially in the arts, friendship is so dependent on matters of roughly equivalent circumstance.

RIGHT AT THE START, Ken Showell showed a painting in the big Whitney "Lyrical Abstraction" exhibit. Nothing good ever happened after that.

Everyone knew he was still painting. But he became an artist's photographer. He'd show up at your house, at your studio, dragging the small cart that contained all his equipment. He'd light, hang, and photograph your pictures, and you'd send the slides and transparencies to your collectors and dealer. Then he'd strap all the lights and reflectors and lenses back down inside a sort of lacquered handmade box and leave. You'd need him about ten times a year. A sandy-haired man with some sweat always on his forehead, from his cart-wheeling.

Talk after was hardest, as with a few sharp snaps of the wrist he disassembled his lenses. We'd started out at the same time, but now I paid him. How do you ignore a thing like that? There were certain questions nobody could ask. The same from both of us, in the narrow hallway by the door. In the embarrassed exchange of goodbye and mutual continued goodwill. Why you and not me?

Ken never asked because he needed our money. And I could not because how do you express to somebody whose expertise you value that you're aware of the small space life has assigned them? And it wasn't awful. All of us hired Kenny. Any field, you told yourself, is staffed and fueled with essential people who started out wanting something else.

He came to New York from Nebraska. I'm looking right now at a painting Ken gave me, of a rose. A small blossom against a gray ground. He was a good painter.

He died of cancer. For a long time he thought it was a pinched nerve, from pulling the cart.

LEO CASTELLI WAS telling his artists, "Paint what you choose, don't worry about money." And André Emmerich was telling us things like, "I need bright-colored paintings. That's what sells. Something red. Red is very, very attractive to clients."

There was the month you heard how André had impatiently advised one of his sculptors, "You have to divorce this woman. She doesn't make parties and she isn't good-looking."

And the sculptor did it. He immediately divorced his wife.

ISAAC WITKIN GAVE UP the Bennington job and the faculty residence. He found a loft in the West Thirties, the oil stain neighborhood. He sort of rocked when he walked around New York, and radiated charisma. His wonderful laugh, opening up his handsome face. He wasn't a great lover. "Fourteen years," Isaac said when we finally slept together. "That's got to be the longest foreplay in recorded history." He went out early the next morning for breakfast provisions. Returned with two orange-and-white bags from Zabar's looking very small in those fists. Isaac ate three big buttery croissants. I sat at the table he'd laid and there was a sudden moment, thinking how much it was like the Bonnards he'd shown me in a huge book one night in Vermont. The silver, the cups and saucers, the pastry, the woman's hands—that morning they belonged to me. Were my hands.

THE RATE OF ATTRITION was beyond belief. Jim Monte was with us. Those nights of cold dunes and the smell of sun-warmed days and afternoons when storms would imprint the sand with shushing, sweet-smelling divots.

He was such a sharp dresser, like a man on a hot streak—tailored suits, great ties, nothing to be concerned about. Jim was a curator at the Whitney. And this felt like the natural progression. To have a person on the inside guiding the museum decisions. And the next thing you know he's been fired by the Whitney. I walked with Isaac into one of the downtown watering places. And there's Jim Monte behind the counter, tending bar, mixing drinks. He had an apron around his waist. I couldn't order a Pinot Grigio from Jim Monte.

I remembered the late afternoon Larry Poons helped me hang my show at Emmerich. The last hours before an opening, when all your tension and ambition peak, your body becoming a tight home for the electricity of various hopes. Jim Monte came up at the opening and announced, "You have two good paintings in this show." I said, "That's two more than you'll ever do." I had a wicked tongue. I guess it was fortunate he got fired.

You need the museum people. They're how you make a leap, from five weeks on the gallery wall to what hangs in a quiet safe room for the public to admire forever. E. A. Carmean helped hang my next Emmerich show. Carmean was at the National Gallery, the founding curator of Twentieth-Century Art. A place like Emmerich is a machine: everybody loves you, everybody wants to be involved with you. You're a package—you and André Emmerich. E. A. was slick and very handsome. Like a youthful prime minister, the face your eye automatically jumps to in a photo. Then E. A. Carmean got fired from the National. For something sad, we heard, like drinking. So then E. A. was at the Fort Worth Museum. Fired. Then he was at the Brooks in Tennessee. Then he dropped the whole thing and became an Episcopal minister. In the *Times*, he made a joke about how the main difference was in the art world you got cheese to go with the bread and wine. Later, he became tangled in a scandal: forgeries of Jackson Pollock and Mark Rothko, my old teacher Tony Smith's great friend. Surprisingly, E. A. was on the wrong side: he'd authenticated the counterfeit Pollock, saying "Your eyes can't lie to you."

These men had their offices and budgets and staffs, people excitedly trailing down the corridors to see what decisions they'd make about the future of art. They had felt themselves to be part of the big story. How did you reconcile not belonging to any story?

THE DEALERS HAD SO MUCH POWER. When you're young what you need is that leg up, that assurance from someone who should know that you are what you think you might be. Darby Bannard came from Princeton. He hit it off with a classmate, Frank Stella, and so there were two people painting on the floor of the dormitory. They got their work to Leo Castelli, who took them both.

"Frank, you will have October," Castelli said to Stella. "November, that's for Darby."

The announcements were all printed. Castelli visited for one last preshow look. And at the last minute he canceled Bannard. Stella's exhibition was a success. Next thing I saw were his black paintings on the curved white walls of the Guggenheim.

THERE WERE SO MANY WAYS TO FAIL. Ken Greenleaf came from Maine, would sit for hours in our loft, picking out chords on his guitar. Half the men around when you pictured them, it was in this strumming hunch.

He loved the sculptor David Smith. There's a magic for young artists to be found in inspiration. Ken skipped college, headed straight for Brooklyn, because it was where Smith had gone. Even lived at the Terminal Works Iron Factory, which is where Smith had welded his first great sculptures. He started showing. After a few years, the *Times* magazine ran Ken on the cover. Reddish hair, bandanna, he had the right look for that moment, plus the steel sculpture.

And he made a mistake. We were all at Stanley Boxer's, standing under the dirty skylight. Archie Rand, a Jewish painter, was wearing something bright-colored. Ken went up to him. "So is that your Jew tie, Archie?" The party guests nearby—I was among them—were stunned. It was a painful moment, which took years for people to forget. Soon after that Ken moved back to Maine. Which didn't really seem to affect his art: he's still very active as a sculptor now.

WHEN ANDRÉ TOLD ME, in the mid-seventies, I was out of the gallery, it didn't especially help to know a number of other young artists were also receiving the same news. I didn't see anybody from SoHo for a long time after that.

It was thirteen years before I had another show. That can happen, a long slump in your career. My son saved the voicemail message in which I phoned to say another gallery was showing my work—"She was just here: I'm in the gallery . . ."—until he gave up that phone number. For years, he carried in his wallet a folded printout of the first *New Yorker* review after I was back.

LARRY POONS LIVED his unimaginable life off Canal. Whenever you climbed the stairs to Poons's fifth-floor studio they'd start regurgitating paint. This effect, liquid paint seeping out his door and oozing down the stairs, usually kicked in when you got to the fourth floor. When he was going for a business meeting Larry would simply bend down and paint his own shoes black.

ANDRÉ CLOSED HIS GALLERY IN 1998. He sold it to someone else. I think it was Sotheby's, which held on for a bit. Now the elegant fifth-floor space in the Fuller Building is a high-end retailer. The commerce arranged no doubt very artfully. The Castelli Gallery is still where it had started, in an elegant town house on the Upper East Side. One of my sons told me he saw the name of one of André's sons in the *Los Angeles Times*. Toby had become powerful in the film business: the head of New Line Cinema, and then chairman of the Warner Brothers Picture Group. The other son, Noah, is a well-known actor. Both look very much like their father: tall, with that commanding forward tilt of the head that seems to request attention. And that charming, incipient smile. André's name is gone from the current art business but not from its memory. But the blue Emmerich sticker on the back of a painting's stretcher bar can still raise its price by at least twenty thousand dollars.

When he came to my first opening in Chelsea at Elizabeth Harris, André looked older. He told me a funny thing: "I knew my standing in the art world had gone way down when I'd call someone and the secretary would ask, "How do you spell the last name Emmerich?"

DAN CHRISTENSEN CAME INTO the city and it had been so long I didn't recognize him at first. There was Dan. Lighter, still with some of his dazzle, in a white linen suit. I knew he'd been sick. And that he'd lost his loft. For a painter, real estate health and physical health are closely allied. Housing is so vital, where you need the big space to generate the work, and then the big space to show and store the work, like the terrifying math that propels a fairy tale. That space of Pollock's at the beach had peace in it. When you don't have a workspace, all you think about all day is what you'd do if you found one. Art is an expensive endeavor to fail at.

I was eating lunch when Dan came into the coffee shop. He did a mediocre version of being surprised to meet. The vitality was gone: his face, close up, especially around the eyes and mouth, looked nibbled away, the smoothness and the excess gone. The parts around his mouth, especially. He said he saw I was in painting clothes, and he wanted to know where my studio was, how I'd gotten it. It seemed so strange to be talking once again with Dan Christensen, three decades later, nearly at the end of everything, about housing. Dan's loft, as you know, had belonged to NYU. And after years and years, they wanted the building back. So there he was. It turned out to be one of the more recent times he was in the paper. Though not in the way we used to be. As a symbol of how changeable the world of art could become.

Later someone showed me the story about him losing his loft. He was now an emblem for how hard the fight to do art could be. "I feel like crying," he said in one story. And, discussing the years when we'd been successes, as "a couple of years where I felt it wasn't a struggle."

Then he brought up the loft thing, as if it were sort of happenstance, accidental, a coincidence of subject matter, like our meeting. "I hear you have a space," he said. His eyes kept their chilly professional watchfulness, the flicker of his old ability. "Is it around here? How do you get this space? I have no place in the city anymore, am out in East Hampton now." I thought about showing it to him, walking from the Empire Diner, and the chat we'd have along the way. Him in that white suit, going slow to accommodate his reduced health, then snapping on the lights in that big studio I love for its quiet and wide windows, its preservation of the best feeling of SoHo, of when I started: freedom. A place that wants you to do your work. It is the thing artists fight for, in every age. And I knew I didn't want Dan's atoms in there, any grains of his presence. So I answered the questions as honestly and noncommittedly as I could.

ISAAC LOVED THE French painter Pierre Bonnard, and there was one time we went to see his favorite painting in New York. We met inside the Guggenheim. It was always wonderful standing next to him—the big burly body and the alert, craggy face. He was wearing his Bennington clothes, jeans and a heavy sweater. I had my cool weather outfit on as usual, jeans and a black turtleneck. "I want to show you that Bonnard we were talking about, the one of the dining room. It's in the Thannhauser Collection," Isaac said.

I knew the picture too. We took the funny little elevator up to the second floor and walked into the Thannhauser wing. We stood in front of *Dining Room on the Garden*. It wasn't large enough to consume your whole field of vision, but still it took you in. Warm blues, greens, and yellow ochres that could only have come from a hedonist's paintbrush. Like any master, Bonnard knew when to stop: before his seductive color turned overripe.

Humbled by the picture at first we said nothing. Then in his deep baritone Isaac broke the silence. "Look how he painted his wife's head, almost as if Marthe were a modern angel." When Isaac died in 2006, a thousand people came out for the memorial—the best turnout he'd had for a while. No one was paying a lot of attention to his work then.

I'M WALKING WITH David through the Met. No paintings by any of us there. We pass the Matisses, the O'Keeffes. And we stand in front of a different Bonnard, a painting of his terrace. And I think of how I am the only person still talking about Isaac, the only person still thinking about Isaac—his beard, his strong welder's hands. I am the only person who remembers that Isaac Witkin really loved the paintings of Pierre Bonnard.

ACKNOWLEDGMENTS

Ed Bendet, a friend from college who now lives in Hawaii, read early drafts of many stories in *Brightening Glance*. He had some wonderful ideas that I put into place. Ed is one of those all-around brilliant people it seems there used to be more of, and who, at the time, were called "cultured."

From the beginning, my friend Ted Wiprud, a classical composer, took an interest. He read many iterations and I could always count on Ted to note what wasn't essential or convincing and needed to be cut.

My saintlike primary doctor George Falk, who reads poetry between patients, shared encouraging words after he read a draft. During my yearly exams we'd had many conversations about literature and Rembrandt, so I was pleased to have his approval.

One day in 2018 Daniel Wenger walked into my painting class fresh from the *New Yorker*, where he'd been a member of the editorial staff. He'd left to become a painter. After we tossed that around, I mentioned some of my new short stories and he agreed to have a look. The next week Daniel arrived back with a marked-up draft that provided invaluable feedback at a pivotal time in my writing process.

Lisa Gerard is a most generous and multitalented young woman who because of her excellent French helped to edit a translation I attempted some years ago. When I learned she was a whiz with computers and totally knowledgeable about formatting issues and other arcane writing practices, her attention to my manuscript made it much more legible.

The brilliant author and *New Yorker* writer Louis Menand asked me to send him *the whole book* when I was simply going to send him one chapter about Clement Greenberg. Menand had recently come out with *The Free World: Art and Thought in the Cold War,* in which there's a riveting chapter about the triumvirate of Pollock, Greenberg, and Krasner. With that shared interest, I was delighted when Louis wrote back that he'd read it all in "one sitting."

Wendy Levinson was the perfect agent for the work, and has exemplified the qualities one hopes to find—sensitivity and good taste, plus patience and stick-to-itiveness.

Thanks as well to Roger Kimball, James Panero, and Benjamin Riley of *The New Criterion,* who published two chapters of *Brightening Glance*—"Alone in a Room" and "Falling Off" in their yearly "Arts" issues: the former in 2023, and the latter in 2022.

Thanks to Jim McCoy and his wonderful team at the University of Iowa Press.

And thanks to my son David, whom I've been talking with about literature since he was six, when he asked about Tolstoy's *The Death of Ivan Ilyich.* As he became a writer David shared much of what he was learning and always kept me thick in books. Over the years we've had endless stimulating conversations about painting and writing—painters and authors. And his encouragement when I first started writing and since—tossing around ideas and words—has been priceless.

Thanks to my son Jonathan, who although he lives across the country has been part of the conversation. With his tremendous memory of childhood and our SoHo loft and the artists he knew, he's provided forgotten details that were essential to the manuscript. Jonathan's logic, and his clarity in general, have improved the final result.

Then and finally, my lifelong thanks to my late father, Bernard George Sutton. Observant, funny, fun, and wise—he wasn't always able to apply what he knew to his own life. But he encouraged me—to try difficult things and to be myself. You could say he was my greatest fan. And, in case by some miracle he is reading this, vice versa.